PERVERTED BELIEFS & STUPID PRAYERS!

REALIGNING WITH THE KINGDOM OF HEAVEN!

by

Janet McKenzie

www.pervertedbeliefsandstupidprayers.com
www.understandingkingdomprecepts.com

ISBN-10:0-9992160-0-7

ISBN-13:978-0-9992160-0-2

Printed in the Unites States of America

DEDICATION

Thy kingdom come, thy will be done on earth as it is in heaven….

..For thine is the kingdom, and the power, and the glory, forever. Amen.

(Matt.6:10, 13)

ACKNOWLEGEMENTS

Utmost thanks to my Abba Daddy God for His extraordinary, fiery love for me and towards me, and His perfecting work in and through me. To Holy Spirit for the sweet fellowship and beautiful communion; for mentoring and imparting good understanding and revelatory truths of His kingdom to me, some of which are mentioned in this Book. And to Jesus, my Savior, friend and brother.

Special thanks also to:

My five amazing children, Nicky, Joshua, Sarah, Elijah and Jayden- for loving me and being constant reminders of how desperately we are all loved of the Father.

The fathers who have imparted many powerful Kingdom principles and precepts into my life; and have prophesied and encouraged me over my life. People like Apostle John Boney, the late Dr. Myles Munroe & Kelley Varner and others who have mentored me over the years.

My editor, Marjorie Kough, for her tireless help in fulfilling God's vision for this Book, for editing, and helping me rework my word.

You the reader, filled with hunger and passion for a deeper knowledge of Yahweh, and a deep desire to see and experience the Kingdom of Heaven in power and demonstration in the Earth. May you be filled with the revelation of the Kingdom of Heaven, and of the Father heart of Yahweh! Amen.

TABLE OF CONTENTS

INTRODUCTION

I was ministering on the Kingdom of God/Heaven before the congregation of my local church. I so remember making a point of correcting some wrong doctrine practiced by the Church; when I felt a strong standard being lifted up within myself. I heard the very clear voice of Yahweh say, "write a book on Perverted Beliefs and Stupid Prayers!" It was so clear and delivered with such conviction that I thought others had heard it also. It sounded as though the Holy Spirit was grieved, even vexed; the Voice was very commanding! I immediately said 'yes" within myself, then almost in one breath I repeated what I had heard to the Body of believers. It was a moment!

Being a bold, radical daughter of Yahweh, I knew I was going to write this book. Yet in the privacy of my head, I attempted a few times to change the name Daddy had spoken to me. It sounded so radical, so confrontational! I thought of the Body of Christ—how the title would look, how the title would sound. Yet I knew deep in my spirit that I had to keep the name. For many times I have felt annoyed and vexed by some things I've heard repeatedly in the Body of Christ, and I felt a duty to bring correction to those people I taught at the time. It just seemed like sometimes things are so upside down in the Church from what the Bible says.

It is from that space this Book speaks; a space of possibility, a space to be a transforming voice crying in the wilderness. Yahweh is so altogether lovely; it is almost an atrocity to let some things go unsaid. We are told in Psalms 82 to *"defend the poor and fatherless: do justice to the afflicted and needy."*

The Oxford Dictionary states God is "the creator and ruler of the

1

universe and source of all moral authority; the supreme being." Essentially god means one empowered to rule. The word god is a common term attributed to deity of any sort. However, in Christianity, the belief is to God Supreme, Omnipotent, Omnipresent and Omniscient.

For the intent of this writing, this author refers to God our Father by some of His names; Yahweh, Jehovah, Yah, Lord, I AM, Father, Ancient of Days! And Daddy: for I have come to know Him as such! Believers are called sons of God; this is not gender related at all; but it speaks of a quality in spirit. Women are also called sons, and men are collectively called the Bride of Christ in Scripture.

In like manner, satan the enemy of the Church, will be referred to most often as the enemy, the devil, the evil one or the adversary. My choice to not capitalize satan's name, or other names by which he is known, is intentional; he doesn't deserve even that much.

PART I

PRINCIPLE OF THE KINGDOM: TRUTH IS LAYERED

CHAPTER 1

UNDERSTANDING KINGDOM PRECEPTS: FIRST THINGS FIRST

Proverbs 22:20-21 states, *"have not I written to thee excellent things in counsels and knowledge that I might make thee know the certainty of the words of truth; that thou mightest answer the words of truth to them that send unto thee?"*

The meaning of the Hebrew word **"excellent" is three-stringed**. There are some fundamental truths—and important concepts which should be kept in mind, as one reads this book. Truth is revealed; and truth unfolds in measures. The three-fold dimensions of the Tabernacle in the wilderness—Outer court, Holy place and the Holy of Holies itself—reveals increasing levels of intimacy in coming to Yahweh our Father with Jesus Himself being the Tabernacle.

One might say this is an old truth because it was written in the Old Testament. As we come into increasing measure of the fullness of the statutes of Yahweh, we want to look at and bring Scripture into present day truth (2 Peter 1:12). Jesus came preaching the message of the Kingdom of Heaven (Matt. 4:17); and He never deviated from it! When asked by Pilate if He was a king, Jesus answered:

Thou sayest that I am a king. To this end was I born, and for this cause came I into the world, that I should bear witness unto the truth. Every one that is of the truth heareth my voice." (Jn 18:36-37)

We know that in His teachings throughout all of the Gospels, Jesus told stories and used beautiful metaphors to illustrate how His kingdom operates. He likened the Kingdom to leaven which a woman used in baking bread, and He tells us that she hid leaven in three measures until the whole was leavened (Matthew 13:33). Jesus also stated that when we, with good hearts, hear and understand the word of God, we become fruitful in measures of thirty, sixty and one hundredfold (Matt.13:23; Mark 4:20). We further see that growth manifests in three-fold measures—first the blade, then the ear, after that the full corn in the ear (Mark 4:28).

This three-dimensional precept permeates all of Jesus' life and ministry, and actually the whole of Scriptures. Jesus is first presented to us as a baby, next we see Him at age twelve as he transitions into manhood in the Jewish tradition; and again, in His full priesthood at age thirty. We might go on concerning the Godhead—Father, Son and Holy Spirit—and man; being a three-part being—spirit, having a soul and living in a body. Then- *there are three that bear record in Heaven—the Father, the Word and the Holy Ghost; and these three are one. And there are three that bear witness in earth, the Spirit, and the water and the blood: and these three agree in one (1 John 5:7,8).*

Based on this principle seen in Scriptures, **it is clear that truth is layered; and so must be looked at in different dimensions.** God himself is never one-dimensional! Scripture states that God's intention for hiding things in a mystery is so that the Church would demonstrate to principalities and powers the many sided, multi-dimensional wisdom of God! (Eph. 3:10). **As such, Scriptures ought to be interpreted in levels of truth**. Even our salvation is never once and for all; we were saved, we are being saved and we shall be saved at Jesus's appearing as the following chapters will unfold.

The issue here oftentimes is that too often popular preaching presents only one dimension of truth. That is not to say that looking at only one level is an error; however: it does mean that a one-level perspective doesn't address the full counsel of God.

A lack of understanding of these ideas and concepts have held multiple believers enslaved in defeatist mindsets, and constantly engaging in war with a foe that has been long defeated. It is from this view of Kingdom paradigm that this book desires to put forth a fresh look at some of the doctrines and beliefs that are incomplete in principle and do not present the full counsel of Father's heart. Many of these have become "sacred cows" within the Church world; and others have deviated from truth; or have mixed truth with error; and are thus perverted. It is only through the Word of God that we are able to put to the test the will of God for our lives. Even the will of God is revealed at different levels: we are told:

Be not conformed to this world but be ye transformed by the renewing of your mind, that ye may prove what is that good and acceptable and perfect will of God. (Romans 12:2).

The Word of God is the medicine for the mind! For like Humpty Dumpty; [in Adam]: man fell on his head! All the king's horses and all the king's men throughout the ages couldn't put Humpty (Adam) together again! Man was created spirit: and spirit is supposed to rule his soul. But in the fall, soul usurped ruler-ship over spirit; and man's flesh submitted to the dictates of his soul. The mind, which resides in the soul of man, sinned; and became like manure for the enemy! Adam [man] thus became carnal in his thinking.

Jesus the Christ was crucified on a hill called Golgatha; which means "the place of the scull [mind/head]. When the crown of thorn pierced Jesu's scull, and His blood flowed, man's mind was now covered by the Blood. Man could once again share in the mind of Christ, positionally: from the Father's end of the covenant. Man could now experience the mind of Christ; on a daily basis; through the renewing of his mind. That responsibility was entrusted to man; as his part of the covenant. Understanding these precepts are foundational to plumbing the depth of the knowledge of God; for these truths demonstrate God's heart.

According to the eternal purpose which God purposed in Christ Jesus our Lord. Ephesians 3:11.

Even now, the Church is beginning to arise out of lethargy to become that transforming voice and light in a darkened world. Man was created spirit; and spirit rules soul when it is aligned with the Word of God. The will of God is known by the mind that has been renewed; and the mind of God/ will of God is revealed in three fold measures as mentioned above (Romans 12:2).

CHAPTER 2

LACK OF KNOWLEDGE
OR THE DEVIL

Perverse: Webster's Dictionary defines perverse as "diverting from the true intent or purpose." Collins English Dictionary says: "deviating from what is regarded as normal, good or proper; marked by a disposition to oppose and contradict; resistant to guidance or discipline; deviating from what is right, proper or good." From the various meanings of perverted, this writer believes that too many issues plague the Body of Christ at large; and over time have blurred the lines of Scripture, causing the Word of God to be perverted; Hosea 4:6 states;

my people are destroyed for a lack of knowledge, because thou hast rejected knowledge, I will also reject thee, seeing thou has forgotten the law of thy God."

The law of the Lord is perfect, converting the soul Psalms19:7

The fear of the Lord is the beginning of knowledge (Proverbs 1:7).

The word destroy means to **perish- to cause to cease-to cut off**. Let us be clear: based on Scripture; knowledge will keep us from being destroyed! It also suggests that wherever there is lack, it is because of the absence of knowledge. When believers are lacking in the understanding of Who Yahweh is, it is because we have ignored Who He says He is! When we ignore the law of God, it is rejection of our Father; to our own detriment, because Father says He will reject us, and we gradually begin to waste away!

So, let us establish from the start; that in the Kingdom of Heaven there is no competition between God and satan! There is no equality and so there can be no competition. Believing otherwise is already perverted! Jehovah is the Creator and the other is a created being! Selah! Knowledge emanates from Yahweh! He alone is Omniscient; [all-knowing]. Knowing Yahweh is having knowledge! Jesus told us in Matthew 4:4 & Luke 4:4

man shall not live by bread alone, but by every word that proceedeth out of the mouth of God!

We ought to live by the Word of God; and we perish from not eating the Word [Bread] of God. This clearly puts the responsibility on believers to get to know our God and Father! Amen! It also removes all that overwhelming responsibility which the Church has placed on satan; he does not get that honor!

The intention of this book is to stir believers into re-examining some of our beliefs, mindsets and behaviors as it concerns God. First: having said that; we need to take the focus from satan, and instead stare into the face of Jesus Christ: the Lover of our souls and the One Who loves us with a fiery everlasting love! Why anyone would want to keep looking at our adversary boggles the mind. After all, what you behold you will become. When we continue to look in the face of Jesus, Scriptures tell us we are:

changed into the same image from glory to glory by the Holy Spirit (2 Corinthians 3:18).

PERISH NOW, OR LATER?

So then, believers perish from ignorance of Who Yahweh is; rather from the devil. Again, ignorance means that something has been ignored! As believers, we are responsible to mature in the knowledge and understanding of our God. The Word of God brings us the knowledge of God; it gives us strength; it causes faith to arise and flood our hearts; and it fills us with the glory of God Himself. Ignoring the Word: Who Yahweh says He is; and ignoring who Yahweh says you are; will cause you to perish gradually. Thus, it is time that we plumb the depth of the knowledge of our God! When Christ is living large within the heart; you become filled up with more and more of the Person, Presence and the nature of God.

Secondly, because our current preaching has been so one

8

dimensional, we have looked toward the future; and have missed the power of the present. **The Kingdom of Heaven is here: it is a now concept!** As we begin to understand the oracles of God, we see Him in unfolding grace and truth; as we become filled with Him!

I am Alpha and Omega, the beginning and the end, saith the Lord; which is, and which was, and which is to come, the Almighty. Revelation 1:8.

He is God now; God of the past and God of the future! Now, when we begin to look at perish or destroy from different levels of truth; we begin to understand, that we were all perishing until Jesus came and rescued us, declaring to be the **Way [to the Father], the Truth[of the Father] and the very Life of the Father (John 14:6).** Without the knowledge of God, you are being destroyed on some level even now. The antidote for this: is getting your mind renewed. Once we received Jesus, we are exhorted and admonished to grow in grace; to renew our minds; and to know the Son. Knowing the Son, is knowing the Father; because the Son is the express image of the Father (Heb1:3); for the Son reveals the Father.

The Word of God is like yeast, it causes a great rise; and acts as a fermenting agent which overtakes the mind and soul; bringing it into alignment with your spirit. It causes the mind to begin to multiply and explode in the things of God, as it reflects the spirit's ruler-ship!

The kingdom of heaven is like unto leaven, which a woman took, and hid in three measures of meal, until the whole was leavened. Matthew 13:33

"Perish" has to do with a gradual wasting away, as if something was being gradually corroded, chipped away and finally destroyed. The movie *The Shawshank Redemption* comes to mind when I think of perish. For years, the prisoner played by Tim Robbins, used a tiny rock hammer to chip away at the wall in his prison cell. It took time, but he created a tiny crater at first; and he continued to chip away at it until eventually, the opening became just a little bit bigger, and bigger and bigger! It was laborious! For years he used that toy-like rock hammer to chip away at that wall, until years later he had formed a hole in the wall big enough that his body could squeeze through! He escaped from that formerly impenetrable prison.

9

We might liken the rock hammer that chipped away at the wall to the "little foxes" that will eventually spoil the vine (Song of Solomon 2:15). Always the enemy of the Church, satan's method is to chip away at believers, subtly and gradually, your whole life; until he gets an opening. satan has been defeated, so he now holds no sway, and no longer possesses any power. Now you have the power and honor; to work with your Father to renew your mind.

As heirs of eternal life, to say that we will perish or be destroyed at the judgement is obviously not the counsel of God! Let's be clear; the Church is being judged now: and believers will not perish at the Judgment seat. The wicked will however! The "judgement" that believers will receive is the measure of rewards; and those will be based on how we have stewarded our lives by the Word of God. So where ever you end up in the Kingdom is a matter of choice for you! In this realm you are in training: so that you might reign with Jesus when He returns to establish His kingdom on earth. Thus, you get to decide where you end up; listen to Luke 19:17

Well done, thou good servant: because thou hast been faithful in a very little, have thou authority over ten cities.

And, behold, I come quickly; and my reward is with me, to give every man according as his works shall be. Revelation 22:12

Another insidious enemy of the Church to which we have become blinded, is the ungodly mindsets and false beliefs that we continue to hold onto concerning the enemy. That is what gradually wears away at your beliefs and your trust in the Lord. It corrodes your understanding! We are told to lay aside *"every weight and the sin which so easily besets us"* (Hebrews 12:2). Although we love to make the word "sin" in that verse plural (sins), the Bible is clear! The "sin" referred to is the lack of faith. Lack of faith in what Yahweh has spoken through His Word! We are responsible to seek after the knowledge of Yahweh. Romans 11:33 says:

O, the depth of the riches of the knowledge of God! How un-searchable are His judgements and His ways past finding out!

DOES satan HAVE ANY POWER?

Jesus destroyed the works of the devil in our lives! (1John3:8).

The works of the enemy, can no longer stick to us; unless we give him the room to do so! satan no longer holds any power over the believer. Our perverted beliefs about satan, however, certainly cause us to gradually waste away. At the core of our issues lies a lack of knowledge of what the Bible says about Jesus, us, and the enemy! The one way to counteract this atrocity; is to acquire and grow more in the knowledge of God; through the Word of God! Another paradigm: using the Word of God, over and over like that rock hammer, causes you to escape satan's prison! Nowhere in the Bible are we told that the adversary causes us to perish/be destroyed.

Our burden then, is to understand the many devices the evil one uses. As in the Garden, one of the adversary's foundational, cunning devices: is the misinterpreting and misunderstanding of Scriptures. This will become more and more evident as you read this book. When the devil looks at you and I, he sees us as the righteousness of God (2Cor.5:21)! That infuriates him! **So, he works fervently to undermine our relationship with our Father**. He does everything and anything he can to deceive you: thwarting Scripture as he did with Eve; to have you doubt our Father. His desire is always to weaken and thwart the image of our Father in your mind.

THE FORGIVENESS FACTOR

First, to reiterate: the devil has no power to cause us to be destroyed! None! What we think of the devil does have the ability to affect us. Jesus did tell us that when there is a lack of understanding concerning the Word of the Kingdom, the wicked one comes and snatches the Word out of the heart (Matthew 13:19). Understanding Kingdom operation then, is very crucial! One of the very fundamental way that he operates against us, **is to use any occasion of unforgiveness on our part, against us!**

to whom ye forgive anything, I forgive also; for if I forgave anything, to whom I forgave it, for your sakes forgave I it in the person of Christ: Lest satan should get an advantage of us: for we are not ignorant of his devices. 2Cor.2:10-11

Since satan can get an advantage against you through unforgiveness; you must work with the Father and keep him out! This is a rather powerful and divine precept; since satan gets to defraud you when you walk in unforgiveness. Plus, when you do not forgive; you are actually stacking up your own transgression in the eyes of the Father. This is a great and powerful kingdom paradigm!

For if ye forgive men their trespasses, your heavenly Father will also forgive you: But if ye forgive not men their trespasses, neither will your Father forgive your trespasses. (Matt.6:15).

Wow! Since **un-forgiveness causes a shifting in the Father's operations towards us**; this must be taken seriously! God is the Supreme King of Heaven and the Universe. Man was created and given rule as kings in the earth. His Son Jesus is the King of kings, and Jesus will set up His Father's kingdom here on Earth!

Then cometh the end; when He shall have delivered up the kingdom to God, even the Father; when He shall have put down all rule and all authority and power...1 Cor.15:24

One exquisite essence and quality of any king; is the power to forgive; to show mercy and kindness! How glorious! How beautiful! What honor! What power! To not forgive belies the very nature of God Himself, and is an affront to His beauty, character and essence. The enemy obviously knows this; and will not fail to use this to devour you. This is the only time in Scripture that there is any mention of satan getting an advantage against believers. This is one precept worth knowing: so we forgive in Christ!

"Forgive us of our debts, as we forgive our debtors.

Not only is this a mandate of our kingdom prayer as Jesus taught (Matt. 6:11-12); it is also a responsibility we have as kings! Our Father is rich in mercy; through which His forgiveness and grace flows. We ought also to do the same; as children of the Most High God! Walking in forgiveness is walking in the mind (consciousness) of Christ. Anything else is the operation of the carnal minded: which is enmity against God and cannot be subject to God! (Romans 8:7). Understanding the devil and his evil deeds, then, is crucial to resisting the wicked one's ploy to make the Word of God of no effect to us. Walking in forgiveness is dismantling the kingdom of darkness one brick at a time! That is a most powerful concept of kingdom life; and it is the heart of our Father! Selah!

CHAPTER 3

EXPOSING THE THIEF

As in Jesus's day, there is a lack of understanding concerning the thief and robber explanation found in John 10. The disciples asked Jesus to explain the parable of the thief and the shepherd and Jesus plainly stated:

Verily, verily I say unto you, I am the door of the sheep. All that ever came before me are thieves and robbers... John10:7-8

Clearly there are many different things that are considered "thieves and robbers." Included among the "all" are our mindsets, belief system, our concepts, opinions, doctrines of men, doctrines of Herod; doctrine of the Scribes and the Pharisees and other religious teachings. These erroneous doctrines, have all been the plan of the enemy to distort the Image of God in the life of a believer! Jesus then qualifies the intention of the thief as coming

only to kill, steal and to destroy (John 10:10).

satan is clearly the master thief. In whatever form his works manifest, **the intention is always to steal the word of faith from your heart, to kill the dream God placed there; thwart your own dreams and desire for the Lord, and then to corrode [destroy] the things of God and render them ineffective in believers' lives.** One of the many devices satan uses, is swaying believers into looking at him; keeping him always in one's consciousness (mind)! he falsely tricks believers into thinking he has power; any amount of power; and having you not understand the Word of the kingdom (Matt.13:19). At this juncture; the carnal mind is in operation. It is from this heart/mind that satan can "snatch the word, since the carnal mind is the meat upon which the devil feeds. This was the curse with which God, Creator Himself cursed the serpent in the garden of Eden (Gens.3:14). he desires to have you to focus on him, for he knows that where your focus goes, your energy also flows. When you focus on darkness and negativity; you will begin to produce more of that kind (negativity). Once you are preoccupied with him and the negatives/darkness in which he traffics; you become changed into his image; and you become blinded to the other things that creep up and take away your liberty in Christ.

satan is the master thief! **The schemes and operations via which his deception manifest, are the thieves and robbers!** Know for sure, that in like manner that there are principles of the Kingdom of Heaven; so are there operations of the kingdom of darkness. It is a ruthless, brutal kingdom, to divide and conquer, to lie, usurp, steal and mislead, and then kill the seed. The seed of the nature of Christ within you! While we have preached the devil as the thief, yet have not thoroughly expounded the ways he operates; the enemy still has believers staring at him, while remaining ignorant of his cunning evil ways. The Chapters of this book are full of expose of satan's operations; hereby dismantling the kingdom of darkness, brick by brick! What the Church falsely believes about him has been a thief that steals our liberty.

Remember in the Garden of Eden that God told Adam clearly that they could eat of any tree in the garden except of the tree of the knowledge of good and evil; or else they would die (Gens.2;16.17). satan came and perverted the words and basically told Eve that God didn't really mean what He said. "What God meant is. . ." and satan twisted their Father's word. The original sin was that Adam questioned his Father's words; much in the same way the enemy has us reading into what God says.

Let me reiterate, the thief is satan. Jesus did say: *thieves and robbers.* **These are the operations of the evil one hidden in many forms and in doctrines, teachings, beliefs and mindsets.** A thief operates behind your back, in secrecy. A robber does it by full, frontal assault, to your person. Nonetheless, the adversary can only devour you or me by way of consent! Scripture makes it clear that he "may" {only} do so to those who permits him to.

be sober, be vigilant: because your adversary the devil, as a roaring lion, walketh about, seeking whom he may devour (1 Peter 5).

The devil cannot devour you or I based on any power or authority he has; or else the Scripture would have said "whom he CAN devour. The devil does not have the **power** to devour us; since he has been stripped of both power and authority! Amen! This is the statement we all must agree with! Jesus has all power! satan has none at all. Zilch! Too often I have heard believers saying that satan has a little power. That, too, is utterly perverse! Jesus declared after His resurrection in (Matt.28:18):

all power is given unto me in heaven and earth; go ye therefore…

Post the resurrection of Jesus, we have been given the very mind of Christ! That is a consciousness which totally agrees with and submits to the Word of God. Jesus admonishes us to live by not just natural bread, but by every Word of God (Matt.4:4)! The Word of God is bread; and it is the food that our spirit and soul feeds on.

For the bread of God is He which cometh down from heaven, and giveth life unto the world.

We know we came to saving knowledge of Christ at repentance from dead works, and faith towards God [the finished works of Christ]; and that it is the gift of God (Eph.2:8)! Believers need not languish anymore between opinions. In Eden; the tempter came and succeeded in having the original couple make a soul-led decision. He has not changed! he still operates to seduce us into having the soul/flesh rule over the spirit.

The Kingdom of Heaven comes equipped with the power of Holy Spirit to empower us to live overcoming spirit led lives! In the Kingdom of Heaven there is multiplied abundance; both of the knowledge and beauty of God! We are not struggling to overcome darkness, we simply turn on the Light. Or better yet; release the Light which is resident within us. We live and walk by the faith of Jesus Christ (Gal.2:20), while giving and receiving the love of the Father shed abroad in our hearts by Holy Spirit. How beautiful!

CHAPTER 4

ZADOK PRIESTHOOD

In order to understand perversion, one must first know and understand the "real." In Ezekiel 44, after the Levitical priesthood had perverted the office, God actually rejected them from ministering to Him! Jehovah then raised up a new order of the priesthood that would minister ONLY to Him. These of the new order were sons of Zadok. They also, were sons of the Levitical priesthood of the day, but had kept the charge of God's sanctuary in a time when the nation of Israel had gone astray.

The word Zadok means righteous: God declared this new Zadok priesthood would: *"teach my people the difference between the holy and the profane and cause them to discern between the clean and the unclean."* (Ezekiel 44:23)

The priesthood of the day had become very corrupt. They had brought into the House of the Lord the very things which Yahweh had forbidden them to do. It was insidious, and they "perished" so gradually that in time Jehovah had to remove them from ministering to Him. **Yet interestingly, that old priesthood still continued to minister to the people; just not to Yahweh (Ezek. 44:7-31). So, two priesthoods began to operate at that time!** When Yahweh chose Zadok to minister to Him; it was a type and shadow of a new priesthood of righteousness under which Jesus Christ would come.

The Levitical priesthood descended from the tribe of Levi, while Jesus descended from the tribe of Judah! Jesus stood *a priest forever after the order of Melchizedek.* (Ps.110:4). Just as the priesthood was changed; the law had to be changed, for in Jesus; righteousness is not according to the law but according to an endless life. (Heb.7:11-17). In much the same manner, many in the Church today

16

have left the first charge of the Lord; and have thus perverted the gospel. Yes, they still minister to the people: but Yahweh forbids them from ministering to Him! There is yet another priesthood: after the order of Melchizedek; who minister to Him: keeping themselves from touching unclean things, and keeping the charge of the Lord.

We are warned that there was coming a time when darkness would cover the earth and gross darkness the people (Isaiah 60:2). There is a "woe" to those who would call light darkness, and darkness light (Isaiah 5:20). **Pure leadership teaches believers the difference between the profane and the holy** as Jesus taught His followers about satan and his operations. Jesus then left us the Word so that believers throughout the ages would not be ignorant of the devil's devices (2Cor.2:11). But Jesus taught His disciples to stare only at His Father! His mission was clear: The Father!

Beloved, perversion comes from the words we speak as much as the actions we do. Mixing the profane with the Holy is that constant emphasizing the works of the devil; staring at him through blame; like weakened victims. **Our responsibility is to usher in the Kingdom of Heaven through our declaration**. When we bring the kingdom in our midst; the will of God is done; and in the Kingdom of Heaven, there is no night; and neither is there any curse there! (Rev.22:3-5). We are destroyed because of a lack of knowledge; not from the devil! (Amos 4:7). Jesus has already destroyed the "works of the evil one; (1John 3:8); and the greater One lives within us (1John 4:4). Amen!

Ignorance of the knowledge of the Father; with over rated attention given to the devil and his actions; causes believers to unwittingly empower him with the power of the fruit of our lips; for we have what we say (Mark 11:22-23). In addition, when believers stare at the devil rather than at the Father; there is an exchange of negative energy towards the believer! We behold only Jesus; we stare only at JESUS! We also become changed into that same image from glory to glory. (2Cor.3:18). Our priesthood is according to the endless life we carry within us: in the Kingdom of God (Lk.17-21). This then is the sacrifice we offer; as priests after the order of Melchizedek! Amen!

CHAPTER 5

THE DUST OF THE EARTH

This principle of the dust of the earth, is one powerful principle which ought to be known and understood by every new convert. It is essential for individual believers to be instructed as to how the enemy works, and how he uses the power of your words. It holds a foundational key to living an overcoming Kingdom lifestyle. Adam (mankind) was created spirit; to be ruled by his spirit; and to receive from his Father, through his spirit. For life on the earth; man was formed from the dust of the earth, so being a man of the dust, Adam was earthly-minded as is all of mankind! (1Cor.15:47-49). Our Father and Creator breathe His life into Adam's nostrils and mankind became a living soul! Man's soul was made to express his spirit; but never to rule over a man's spirit.

FROM THE FALL TO CALVARY: A SYNOPSIS.

Adam was given a mandate to dress and keep the garden of God. His responsibilities included: keeping and managing the consciousness or mind of Christ [Eden]. When Adam fell metaphorically on his head like Humpty Dumpty; his soul which houses the mind is what sinned; and became carnal in thinking, and competitive enemy to the mind of God! God is Spirit, and He communicates through His Spirit to man's spirit. **Our Father just would not put up with the rule of soul/flesh over spirit so the light went out in man's spirit.** For soul absolutely could not be allowed to continue to rule over spirit. Due to this major breach (sin), man's body was now subject to the dictates of his soul, and became exposed to diseases and all kind of maladies. Father shed the blood of an animal and made coats of skin, and clothed Adam and Eve, to cover the breach of their sin (Gens3:21).

Adam and Eve: already blessed by Jehovah, had to pay the consequences of violating Jehovah's precepts nonetheless. As a result, Jehovah cursed the ground from which Adam came for Adam's sake. Adam would now have to toil for his living, rather than live by the inspiration of his mind! Now through Adam: man's soul-led mind being formed from the ground, would also always be unfruitful; and always bear the proverbial "thorns and thistles." (Gens.3:18). Eve would become subject to the mind of her husband; his desires, his will, his urges, and he would now rule over her! Eve was to have sorrow of mind, and would languish in pain in bringing forth the seed of her womb. God does not speak to, or through man's carnal mind, He speaks only through the spirit of man!

The serpent being cursed; was relegated to crawl on its belly **and eat dust** (Genesis 3:14). Since the soul/mind of man **came from dust; the carnal mind [soul led] was cursed as food for the devil! Since the fall of man, the only thing that the serpent eats from, and the only place the serpent lives; is the carnal mind of mankind. This is a very powerful precept to understand as believers, specifically in regards to how the evil one operates and manipulates the fleshy mind of individuals. This too is especially fundamental, in the saving of one's soul.**

For to be carnal minded is death; but to be spiritually minded is life and peace. Because the carnal mind is enmity against God; for it is not subject to the law of God, neither indeed can be. So then those that are in the flesh cannot please God. (Romans 8:6-8)

This is crucial in understanding how the devil operates; lest we give him power he doesn't have! For oftentimes, believers have thought and said; that satan can read your mind. The devil cannot read your mind! No way! **A mind which is stayed upon God; a mind which has been renewed; cannot be penetrated by the enemy**. On the other hand; when a person is ruled by his carnal mind and not his spirit; then that man cannot and will not be able to intuit the things of God, because the carnal mind is arch enemy to God! **It only appears like satan can read one's mind; because that person is trafficking in the things of his fallen soul; [carnal mind] and is thus not subject to God's rule.** This is exactly where satan lives and feeds. What he feeds on is the fleshy, ungodly things which we utter from our lips: which are contrary to God's will and His ways. This is the devil's domain. Jesus plainly told us:

the kingdom of heaven is likened unto a man which sowed good seed in his field; but while men slept; his enemy came and sowed tares among the wheat, and went his way

The carnal mind is the devil's domain; it is his house. This key of the principle of the dust of the earth has not been taught to believers enough, so far too many believers languish between opinions; one minute, confessing Jesus, and the next minute thinking and saying the devil has power. Through ignorance of this precept, satan appears to know so much, and to wield power that he actually does not have! He is the father of lies and prince of darkness. If you are breathing at all, you have experienced runaway thoughts trafficking through your mind. These are thoughts which are contrary to even your own will; thoughts which at times might even surprise you!

As a new believer, I remember hearing my own "thoughts" cursing at me; lying and condemning me many times! I heard Kenneth Copeland say one time that what the mouth speaks, the mind hears and will eventually believe. I then began to open up my mouth, and use the Word of God to counteract the thoughts I heard cursing at me. Although I myself did not yet know of this principle of the dust of the earth; I obeyed and radically, repeatedly declared that I am the righteousness of God in Christ. As I increasingly spoke the Scriptures; my thoughts began to subject themselves to the Word of God! Those negative voices began to wane and weaken! Praise God!

That is the principle of *faith cometh by hearing and hearing by the word of God! On the c*ontrary, fear and unbelief come by hearing and hearing the negative words of the kingdom of darkness. What is crucial to know is; **negative, random, evil thoughts which flashes through your mind, come from the carnal mind. That little negative voice always negating what you set your mind to do; that is the fallen un-renewed soul- devil's food;** coming from the carnal mind! You must answer these with God's Word! Always!

Know this: you do not have two minds! You and I were born

carnal in thinking, after the likeness of Adam at the fall, for we did bear the image of the first Adam. *In the same manner that we have borne Adam's image, so we must bear the image of the second Adam (1 Cor. 15:47-49);* who is the Lord Jesus. In Adam, under the curse, our carnal minds would be unfruitful (Gens.3:18). Thus, we must also embrace the truth that we now have the mind of Christ! Amen! For when Jesus's head was bloodied from the crown of thorns which pierced his skull; it is symbolic of Jesus's whole soul being redeemed from the curse initiated by Adam.

And when they had platted a crown of thorns, they put it upon His head... (Matt.27:29; Mark15:17; John 19:2)

So, the devil loves when and if a believer says that he can read your mind! Just that utterance already: is carnal in thinking and contrary to God's will! That is utter nonsense; and this is why, the principle of the dust of the earth is crucial to understand his operations. **This is that "law of sin and death the Apostle Paul talked about in Romans 8:2.** This is a really, key, foundational way the enemy works, having believers think that he holds some sway over us! The following chapters will begin to unravel just how satan seduces us through the carnal mind.

Now through Jesus, the second Adam, (1 Cor. 15:45), our spirits once again have rule over our souls! That was Yahweh's original intent! Scripture exhorts us (1 Cor. 2:16), that *we have the mind of Christ.* Based on covenant, the blood of Jesus brought our spirit, soul and body back into right alignment; and it is the wisdom of God! Experientially, believers flesh this out, when we walk in the Word of God, and empowered by Holy Spirit! In regeneration, the light in man's spirit which had gone out in Adam; was now re-illuminated by the Light of Jesus the second Adam! Amen! The Bible says believers are now called the light of the world (Matt 5:14); and it says of Jesus.

That was the true Light, which lighteth every man that cometh into the world (John 1:9). Amen!

CHAPTER 6

THE LEAVEN OF
THE PHARISEES

Jesus once told his disciples to beware of the leaven of the Pharisees (Matthew 16:6; Mark 8:15; Luke 12:1).His disciples mistakenly believed that Jesus meant natural bread; because they were about to feed a multitude, and had forgotten to bring bread with them. Jesus reminded them of the miracles they had already experienced in feeding multitudes. Leaven here is used for doctrine; (Matt. 16:12); the erroneous doctrine that was being preached by the religious leaders of the time. Jesus called it hypocrisy; and cautioned them about it. What then is that doctrine that we should be wary of?

Dictionary.com states: "leaven is a substance like yeast that is added to dough, and causes it to ferment and rise".

The leaven of the Pharisees is any reasoning in one's heart how to please God through the works of the soul. It depends on the flesh; on one's own understanding. It is ego-centered and self-righteous at its core. They sought after signs, questioned Jesus about His healings, and they clamored over traditions like handwashing, healings on the Sabbath, and whether healing was from God or the devil! The Pharisees held themselves far more righteous than others, based on their works. Yet Jesus called them hypocrites. Jesus said:

For I say unto you, that unless your righteousness shall exceed the righteousness of the scribes and Pharisees, ye shall in no wise enter into the kingdom of heaven (Matt.5:20).

Jesus made it plain in His Sermon on the Mount; when He taught the principles of the Laws of the Kingdom of Heaven. In essence, this doctrine fashions God after man's image, and like yeast; rises undetected, bombarding the mind and filling it with fleshy, soulish, toxic thoughts. The author of it is, of course, our adversary the devil.

Understanding the Leaven of the Pharisees is crucial as you work out your salvation and save your own soul! It exposes the very serious danger of depending on soul to lead you, instead of spirit! It exposes how the insidious fermenting of error, toxic negativity and darkness generates from the un-renewed mind. It also presents the most crucial and deceitful way the enemy devises his cunningness.

beelzebub is one of the many names for the devil; and beelzebub is the prince of devils (Matt 12:24). The word means "lord of the flies." If nothing else, the enemy realized that the sons of men are born as kings! Kings decree matters; kings have authority, and the word of a king is mighty. This was put on display when our Father **watched and allowed Adam to name the animals** (Gens.2:19); without any questioning from God. satan saw the authority of the spoken word in action. Additionally, he knows how to use the power of agreement (Matt.18:19): so he got Eve to agree with him, by doubting the Word of her Father (Gens. 3:4).

Since the adversary was stripped of all his power upon Jesus' resurrection, **he devises to suck the power from God's sons and daughters.** Since the enemy is the master both of manipulation and misdirection; his intent is to undermine Jesus's Bride. So if satan can get a believer to agree with, and speak any lie against God, the Holy writ, or any one thing concerning the promises of God, then he has usurped your power. The power lies in your words! Firstly, what you say manifest; good or bad! **When you speak negatively, he has you! For your un-renewed mind/soul is ruling in that moment, and that is his food. Your negative words attract him; and he comes as beelzebub; and uses his "flies" to come and multiply quickly around those negative words**. Watch this process of how Beelzebub operates: **it is imperative that you begin to become aware of this operation of the enemy!**

Have you ever put a bit of rotten or uncooked meat in your garbage bin? You even covered the top before going on your way. Yet in little time a great swarm of flies gather around making annoying noises and you wonder where in the world did they come from, and so quickly? Or perhaps a piece of fruit is left on the kitchen counter for a little while, and before you know it, there are fruit flies hovering around. You even wonder where they came from, especially since the windows in your house are closed? This is a great picture of how satan operates as beelzebub; lord of the flies! He quickly multiplies the negatives, and like leaven, causes a great swelling of those negatives- within one's mind. Then before you know it, you are bombarded with toxic, negative, ugly thoughts!

Those negatively energized words cause a leavening effect in your mind; and in the same manner that those flies quickly appear and multiply; so it is, that you begin to experience rapidly increasing negative thoughts. These rising toxic thoughts have a "mind" of their own, bombarding and multiplying more and more negatives in your soul! Until they become a stronghold, as your soul becomes bathed in toxicity. The danger is having you begin to believe that you are right in your own eyes; hence the self- righteousness! Those carnal thoughts are not subject to God at all (Roms.8:6).

Researchers have actually found that whenever you have a negative thought: the brain will actually make and lay down new nerve pathways to support that negative thinking. Even social scientists know that what you speak about is that which will manifest in your world. It is called the Law of Attraction. Before science was, Jesus is! As in the Garden when he influenced Eve to second guess the word of her Father, **he ruthlessly desires to have us agree with him in our thinking and to speak it with our lips.** The devil was, and remains a bitter usurper to God's sons. He tried it with Jesus at His temptation but failed. He still tries it with believers; every single day! Then he uses it against you to utterly crush and annihilate you; and build the kingdom of darkness.

The devil does see believers as the righteousness of God; and he hates that! Let me reiterate; **as kings, you carry power in your words; you were given authority to speak and it would manifest!** This is potent! The devil then, devises constantly to have you speak contrary to the Word of God! **The moment you say it out of your mouth, satan latches on to your authority and steals it! Satan thirst for power; and word have energy, and he uses whatever he can get, no matter how minute it might seem.**

a little leaven leaveneth the whole lump." (1Cor. 5:6; Gal. 5:9).

Perverted, negatively energized thoughts and words, comes from, and is food for the kingdom of darkness! They are already produced from the un-renewed soul: the carnal mind where the enemy lives and feeds. When you speak any such words, any rotten thinking, no matter how minute, creates an opening for beelzebub. **Negative words act like a fermenting agent[leaven], and causes a great rise of negativity!** It is to this end that Scriptures tell us;

death and life is in the power of the tongue, and those who love it will eat the fruit thereof. (Pro. 18:21)

Know that satan uses your negative "soulish" words to work against you! This is one major way the devil uses this dark principle against us, and believers can no longer afford to be ignorant of this anymore. You absolutely must walk in the understanding of this disgusting dark mess! **The Leaven of the Pharisees is a mindset which allows the soul rather than the spirit to rule you. It dangerously overwhelms your mind, leading you into captivity.** When this continues; it causes you to speak and think even more negatives; **and you start to believe they are your own thoughts; because you are thinking them!** The carnal mind which already resists the Word of God, and cannot even be subject to God's word; now wages a wicked war against you: causing major strongholds to be formed in your mind.

Like flies swarming over rotten meat; beelzebub yet causes the rising negativity to multiple even more, and overtake your thoughts; leaving you toxic and at his mercy. You begin to see darkness as light; wrong as right; in your own eyes! What is crucial here is that as believers we must realize the power of the spoken word! The power that is in your mouth! Amen! beelzebub feeds on your carnal thoughts, takes them over and feeds them back to you swamping you with even more negatives thoughts.

For though we walk in the flesh, we do not war after the flesh: For the weapons of our warfare are not carnal, but mighty through God to the pulling down of strongholds. Casting down imaginations and every high thing that exalteth itself against the knowledge of God, and bringing into captivity every though to the obedience of Christ: and having in a readiness to revenge all disobedience, when your obedience is fulfilled." (2 Cor.10:2-6)

Any doctrine which fashions **God according to man's mindset; rather than the Word of the Kingdom acts against the believer; and causes multiplication of falsehood in the mind**. Once our knowledge of God is weakened through doubts and questionings, the wicked one truly begin to get a strong hold! Then he mercilessly digs in; and bombards you even more with multiplied, negatives thoughts. The operations of beelzebub within the Leaven of the Pharisees is an insidiously, wicked doctrine which works cunningly against the minds of believers. **The Church must be both aware of, as well as be mindful of this perverted, poisonous device of the enemy,** and be ready to truly avenge and resist it through the Word of God. The Word of God is absolutely the most powerful of Leaven! It causes powerful multiplication of good; it multiplies and overwhelms the poisonous leaven of the soul. Matt.13:33

The kingdom of heaven is like unto leaven, which a woman took, and hid in three measures of meal, till the whole was leavened.

Jesus warned His disciples to beware of this doctrine! It is therefore expedient that we understand it! Like rat poison, it is 99 % corn, [it sounds like God] yet it is the 1% strychnine added to it, which makes it truly poisonous!

CHAPTER 7

THE TONGUE

T
he Church has been swatting away at a defeated devil, sermon after sermon, and in conference after conference. Scripture says: *"every wise woman buildeth her house: but the foolish plucketh it down"* (Pro.14:1).The Church has often been foolish in things said and done in the name of God: and has been guilty, although inadvertently; of destroying the beauty of God's house, through ignorance.

Perverse means **"deviating from that which is proper, right or good."** The word perverse might prompt you to think of cursing, foul or dirty language. Yet if we are to look at perverse based on the actual meanings stated above; and in light of Scriptures; we get a different paradigm of God's heart. Believers are not uttering curse words as the world knows them: nonetheless the Church too often, like ancient Israel; have deviated from right, through rejecting the very word/law of God!

We ought to be mindful of our conversation; for too often our lips put us into the realm of perversion as far as the Word of God is concerned. We know that the enemy was stripped of all authority and all power (Matt. 28:18) upon the resurrection of Jesus! The one big question is; **does the devil have power to destroy us; or is it our misguided, rotten thinking and speaking that empowers the enemy?** Proverbs 18:20-21 states that

death and life is in the power of the tongue…

evil communication corrupts good manners. Awake to righteousness and sin not; for some have not the knowledge of God 1Cor.15:33-34

So whatever fruit you are eating is based on your tongue. The

Word of God tells us that **our tongue has the ability to create death for us as well as life. Nowhere is there any mention of the devil**! Incredibly, the Bible is filled with this principle, yet it appears we have been sleepwalking since our most popular preaching is highly devil-centered. **There is an overwhelming tendency to shift blame, and accept little responsibility, for things which happens in our lives.** This is unscriptural and perverse. We were created in the image and likeness of God, speaking spirits and what we say have power in either direction! We are admonished:

and they that love it shall eat the fruit thereof.

Now it seems that believers of God should not have to be admonished about such things; yet God tell us that we manifest the fruit of our tongue! In the disciples' prayer Jesus taught us to say: *"deliver us from evil, for thine is the kingdom."* (Matt.6:13). Evil indicates our enemy satan of course! Another paradigm of evil means **useless, empty, futile. In God's eyes, words which belie the power of Yahweh, are evil! Faithless words, and those which testify to, and enlarge the kingdom of darkness are evil.** The Kingdom of Heaven is the solution: for it delivers us from evil!

When the Church turns around and too often, in our preaching; cast blame on a defeated foe; that is an evil! Now let me be very clear here! **There is a real devil! Jesus our Savior through His death and resurrection; have however already delivered us**:

for this purpose the Son of God was manifested, that He might destroy the works of the devil (1John 3:8). Amen!

As kings, **our salvation involves taking responsibility every time, for the words and deeds which we do.** When we miss the mark/sin; we do have an advocate Who is Jesus (1John 2:1). Amen! We get to use the tools of confession and repentance; given to us through God's grace, mercy, and love: to continue to run the race. The **constant dialogue about what the enemy is currently doing rather than what our Lord has done becomes empty in itself!** You have such power in your tongue; that those kinds of speaking; enlarges the dark kingdom in your life. As in the beginning; the mandate for us; as kings; is still to **"dress and keep"** the garden. Truth is layered: there was the physical garden; yet on a deeper

28

level; **the garden is a "state of being; the consciousness of the mind of Christ.** On yet another deep layer of truth, **the Garden is the Kingdom of Heaven on Earth**! We are called to this, and we do greatly err when we do not steward our words! The Kingdom of Heaven is the realm of God's total Lordship

Put away from thee a froward mouth, and perverse lips put far from thee. (Pro. 4:24).

That word froward in Hebrews means "distorted; crooked." It is a sorrowful thing that the Church has been propagating this perverseness of the devil and overplaying his involvement in believer's life! **Believers should not be rebuilding with our mouths the very things which Jesus suffered and died to destroy.** Did Jesus totally dismantle the kingdom of darkness or not? Categorically yes! He did! He even made a show of them openly, triumphing over them in it (Colossians 2:15). This is the picture of Jesus displaying satan before Almighty God and His Father; the King of Heaven!

Whoso offereth praise glorifieth me, and to him that ordereth his conversation aright, will I shew the salvation of God (Psalm 50:23).

Salvation involves, healing, joy, deliverance, prosperity, peace, victory, abundance, safety and more! When you see that things are not manifesting in your life; it is because of you not ordering your words aright! **That is one powerful kingdom key! As you are intentional with your words, God does His part to fulfill what you say! This is co-laboring!** As you are calling *those things which be not as though they were* (Romans 4:17); for you believe, and so you speak (2Cor. 4:13). This is the spirit of faith! For we *walk by faith and not by sight (2Cor5:7)*! Plus, having been made justified by the Blood of Jesus, you now *live by faith* (Romans 1:17).

Faith always speaks! You are a speaking spirit with creative power in your mouth. You are made in the image of God, and after His likeness. Do it! Open up your mouth, and declare the Word of Almighty God and put to naught the devices of the enemy. Amen!

CHAPTER 8

THE PRINCIPLE
OF AUTHORITY

Another powerful paradigm to look at is the **principle of Authority.** Yahweh gave Adam authority as a king on the earth even while we were yet in Adam's loins; and we get to see how God initiated him into this role.

And out of the ground the Lord God formed every beast of the field and every fowl of the air; and brought them unto Adam to see what he would call them: and whatsoever Adam called every living creature, that was the name thereof." (Genesis 2:19)

There was no debate; there was no discussion from Yahweh; just pure, loving trust! How utterly beautiful; how marvelous! Amen! This is the model of delegated authority, and beautiful trust! However, Adam, so much like all of us, failed to see how much trust Yahweh had placed in him. You and I, being made in the image and after the likeness of the Godhead, are speaking spirits as well, so whatever we say will manifest.

Genesis opens with the Supreme God Who spoke Light into existence! Light is a manifestation of God's essence; light is energy! Thus as kings on the earth, what we speak ought to be evidence of the light of God, for we are to be imitators of Christ (Ephesians 5:1).**As light of the world (Matthew 5:14); we manifest that we are light; when we also speak light into existence!** So, we must become mindful of what comes from our mouth. Jesus said: *"the words that I speak are spirit and life (Jn.6:63).* We are joint heirs with Jesus, and as He is, so are we in the world (1John 4:17). The words we speak are energy and life also: and we are creating realms of possibilities every time we open our mouths. Fact is, we have been creating possibilities, but on the dark side. We cannot get away from it! We create with our mouths whether we want to or not. We are kings!

Having said all that, it is apparent that we have too often been furthering the cause of the kingdom of darkness by our manner of speaking. **We were given delegated power and authority; in our mouths! This is the power satan uses; your power!** Can you now see how the enemy uses his cunning devices on you when you walk ignorant of this powerful concept? The enemy actually wants believers to think and say that he has power, so he can usurp **your** authority, latch onto **your** words and overtake **your** mind. Since the Cross; we have been given the mind of Christ (1Cor.2:16); and we manifest it when we declare God's Word!

These are powerful kingdom paradigms. **In order to bring what you desire into manifestation, you must be intentional about speaking it into being**! This is an act of saving one's soul and this is the heritage of every believer in Christ. To think or speak anything otherwise is perverse in the eyes of God; yet God is merciful and longsuffering towards us. Regardless of the situation, believers have power to speak those things that are not as though they were; because you co-create by speaking!

We having the same spirit of faith, according as it is written, I believed and therefore have I spoken; we also believe, and therefore speak (2Cor.4:13).

Now let's be clear, there are two kingdoms that are constantly in conflict—the Kingdom of Heaven and the kingdom of darkness. Because we believers live in this realm of earth, we feel and experience constant buffeting and the continuous stress of satan's kingdom jockeying for position. The Kingdom of Heaven is the only solution! We get to access it; with our mouths; through declaration; and bring it into our daily lives and it matters not what the enemy does! The Kingdom of Heaven overwhelms it! So, when faced with any kind of opposition, trial or turmoil; we are given the weaponry of the spoken word; to obliterate every obstacle! Jesus died to bring us His Father's Kingdom; and Jesus the Son made us family. Yahweh's word is true; and it never fails!

for verily I say unto you, that whosoever shall say to this mountain, Be thou removed, and be thou cast into the sea: and shall not doubt in his heart, but shall believe that those things which he saith shall come to pass: he shall have whatsoever he saith Mark 11:22:

When the deceitful one approached Eve, she told it to Adam her husband. They both failed to recognize the power and authority they had been entrusted with; and gave their authority over to the deceiver, thereby committing treason against the Eternal Supreme King, and Kingdom! Adam ignored his status as a king of the earth much in the same way we do as kings and priests in the Earth today. We give in to the deceiver so many times by failing to walk in our dominion! Remember we are told in Psalms 115:16,

the Heavens are the Lord's: but the earth He has given to the children of men."

For the wisdom of the Father was already set in place. **His Son as a man of the earth was already set to come and recover what the deceiver, satan, would take from God's man, Adam!** It was not an afterthought—it had been planned from before man was even formed; from when the world was being founded. Scripture says:

…the Lamb slain from the foundation of the world. (Rev 13:8).

The Lord wouldn't, and couldn't, spar with satan because, being Supreme God, He is obviously above satan. They are unequal! Only bullies pick on those weaker than themselves. The Ancient of Days sent His Son Jesus; being in the fashion and form of man, to crush and totally dismantle satan's kingdom; and did He ever!

For this purpose the Son of God was manifested, that He might destroy the works of the devil! (1John 3:8)

The first man Adam was made a living soul; Jesus the last Adam as a quickening spirit (1 Cor. 15:45). It was part of God's plan! **The Son of God became the son of man, so that the sons of men might become sons of God.** How powerful, how precious and how cool is that! It was all for Love's sake! Amen! As we get a fresh impartation of the Lord's fiery passionate love for us, it behooves us to learn of Him, and get to know Him. We actually show our love for Him, when we delve into knowing more about Him.

CHAPTER 9

A WHOLESOME TONGUE

"A wholesome tongue is a tree of life . . ." (Proverbs 15:4)

J esus, the Pattern Son; models for us the responsibility we have as little gods on the Earth (Ps.82;5; John 10:34). It is a marvelous picture of how we get to co-labor with the Lord; and an essential way of how we get to live the overcoming life.

Have faith in God. For verily I say unto you, That, whosoever shall say unto this mountain, be thou removed, and be thou cast into the sea; and shall not doubt in his heart, but shall believe that those things which he saith shall come to pass, he shall have whatsoever he saith." Mark 11:22-23.

Whatever issue believers face, we have been given many keys with which to overcome the devil! Proof is right there in the Word and we can no longer ignore that! Interestingly Jesus tells us to first say **"be removed", then: do not doubt, but believe what you say;** then we will see a manifestation of what we say. Interestingly, He **didn't say that we should believe it first. Now** He never said **that we should say what we believe; but rather that we should believe what we say. Saying or declaring is paramount!** Glory to God!

What you say with your mouth your soul will come to believe! Then you will your mind to not doubt, but believe what you say! Powerful mind training! Your unconscious mind/soul hears what your lips say, and begin to form feeling, ideas, concepts, moods and auras around those words! This is a key to **Renewing the mind!**

In the beginning, God Almighty moved over darkness and spoke light into being. As a believer, you ought now speak the same! You speak of the victory and glories of our King; as your mouth overflows with grace; extoling the mercies of our Lord and God; the truth of His Kingdom and dominion! As the Psalmist David declares:

My heart overflows with a noble theme, I recite my verses for the King. My tongue is like the pen of a ready writer Psalms 45:1

POSITIVE EXPECTANCY:

A very powerful precept to get good things to happen in your life **is to create a legacy, a stronghold of positive expectation. This comes from the Word of God; it is the antidote to destroying strongholds of the carnal mind.** The flesh [carnal mind] pushes out negative expectancies; and if you listen to yourself; you will hear the negatives coming out. You will hear the fears; the doubts and the contrary speaking: all opposites to what the Word says.

The Word of God tells you the good things of God, and of who you are! Amen! You are above only and not beneath; you are the apple of your Father's eyes; you were created for dominion; greater is He that is in you than he that is in the world: and you can do all things through Christ Who gives you strength! No weapon formed against you shall prosper; and every tongue that rises against you; you shall condemn! The list goes on and on!

This then is the expectation on which to build your thoughts, and starve your doubts and fears. Although, at times, and because of the constant buffeting from the dark kingdom; you might experience discouragement. Frustration from worry, stress and tiredness, might cause you to react and **"miss the mark".** Yet you can with your mouth create the food from which your own soul will feed.

When thoughts of fear and negativity come; **your tongue; speaking the wholesome Word of God will create a tree of life, from which you will be able to eat and feed continually.** As you do and continue to speak the Word of God to the fearful negative thoughts; the anointing which is on the Word, will destroy the yoke of the fear and negativity! In time, the words you keep declaring will start popping up from your mind without you even consciously thinking them! This is the tree of Life, the Word of God, which will sustain you! A wholesome tongue is a tree of life! Praise God!

Moses's story comes to mind. Being raised in Pharaoh's palace but having his sister and mother as his caregivers; Moses no doubt had the expectancy that his life had some meaning, and that Jehovah would use him in a purposeful way. At forty years old, he defended one of his people by killing an Egyptian and burying him in the sand. His deed was discovered, and so Moses had to leave town speedily! For forty long years, he was in obscurity in the desert; until he had a Burning Bush encounter with Yahweh in Exodus 3:2.

Fast forward to the Red Sea after Pharaoh had finally released Israel under great duress, and after many mighty miracles and wonders! Now the Egyptians were in hot pursuit, and the Red Sea loomed in front of them! The whole nation saw Pharaoh coming and began to fear greatly! They began to complain against Moses and ultimately against God in Exodus 14:10-12. They even said:

For it was better for us to serve the Egyptians, than that we should die in the wilderness [verse 12].

Even after the wondrous signs with which Jehovah had brought them out of Egypt; the nation had negative attitude and expectancy! Much like we do at times. That Red Sea represented the realm of the Supernatural for Israel; but they had such negative outlook that they couldn't help but complain. We all have doubts, at least on some level as we grow in God's grace; but you must realize that your negative attitude and expectancies will work to help create the very experience! Complaining is always filled with negatives!

For as a man thinketh in his heart, so is he (Pro.23:7).

However, Moses the man of God had over time so developed a good positive attitude and expectation that he declared:

Fear ye not, stand still, and see the salvation of the Lord, which He will shew you today: for the Egyptian ye have seen today, ye shall see them again no more forever; the Lord shall fight for you, and ye shall hold your peace. Exodus 14:13-14.

Yet right after Moses uttered those calming words; I AM answered:

wherefore criest thou unto me? Speak unto the children of Israel that they go forward...

Moses must have been crying out in his heart to God then! Yet his utterance was positive and declarative; as the words of a king. Having already declared *"standstill and see the salvation of the Lord,"* Yahweh then instructed Moses's faith on how to mix his faith words with his actions.

and lift thou up thy rod, and stretch out thine hand over the sea, and divide it...

We know the rest of the story! The same God Who had wrought a great and mighty deliverance before; caused the Red Sea to part and Israel passed through on dry ground! Hallelujah! The power of positive expectancy! We can go on about Joseph in prison; always believing; and always expecting his dreams to manifest regardless of the circumstances.

Then there was Paul and Silas: badly beaten and heavily chained in the inner prison, they offered up praise and thanksgiving, causing their chains to be loosed so they could go free in Acts 16:25-26. The power of positive expectancy! The centurion who stated to Jesus: *"but speak the word only and my servant shall be healed"* (Matt.8:8) or the woman with the issue of blood who said within herself

if I may but touch His garment, I will be made whole.

What about the Canaanite woman whose daughter had a devil; she pressed into Jesus when she was told that *"it is not meet to take the children's bread and cast it to the dogs." She countered* with her declaration:

Yes, Lord but the dogs under the table eat of the children's crumbs. (Matt.15:25-28; mk.7:25-30! Hallelujah!

All these people had such positive expectancy! They mixed their words with their actions (James 2:17-18); spoke with their mouths, and they believed what they said, not what their circumstance dictated! Amen! They surely received what they said. SELAH!

CHAPTER 10

HOW TO SAVE THE SOUL!

At Calvary the shedding of Jesus's blood totally remitted mankind's sin. **The spirit of man being regenerated by Holy Spirit; assumed it ruler-ship position over the soul** as Yahweh had created it to be! Our bodies also will be saved at the appearance of Jesus:

Behold, I show you a mystery: we shall not all sleep; but we shall all be changed; in a moment in the twinkling of an eye, at the last trump; for the trumpet shall sound, and the dead shall be raised incorruptible, and we shall be changed. 1Cor.15:51-52.

Nowhere in Scriptures is there any mention of the spirit of man sinning! The spirit did not sin; but soul sinned: and mankind's body basically succumbed to the dictates of the soul. Ezekiel 18:20 says

that the soul that sins shall surely die.

On this side of Calvary, your spirit has been born again through the precious blood of Jesus! In the very same manner that baking soda causes dough to greatly rise, Jesus's blood acted as that fermenting agent: powerfully causing a great transforming rise within the soul It was through the Blood of Christ, that Holy Spirit came with power and authority! Once again, man's spirit has rule over the soul, but the soul yet needs to be saved!

For the life of the flesh is in the blood: and I have given it to you upon the altar, to make an atonement for your souls; for it is the blood that maketh an atonement for the soul. Lev.17:11

Father God has done His part of the covenant through the shed blood of Jesus. Amen. Covenantally you become saved as Heb.6:1 says; through "repentance from dead works, and faith towards God.

THE POWER & RESPONSIBILITY OF CO-LABORING

God shed the blood of His Son; and now we get to appropriate the blood of Jesus, experientially; as our covenant responsibility with our Father. Once your spirit was re-generated, it retained its ruler-ship position over your soul! Importantly though, in order to rightly express your spirit which receives from Holy Spirit; the soul yet needs to be realigned with the Word of God. **Scriptures, does not mention that God saves our soul.** What is both inferred as well as mentioned**, is that you get to save your soul as your part of the covenant!** The Apostle Paul admonishes in Phil.2;12-13

Work out your own salvation with fear and trembling; for it is God which worketh in you, both to will and to do of His good pleasure

I beseech you therefore, brethren, by the mercies of God, that ye present your bodies a living sacrifice, holy, acceptable unto God, which is your reasonable service. And be not conformed to this world: but be ye transformed by the renewing of your mind, that ye may prove what is that good, and acceptable, and perfect will of God. (Romans 12:1-2)

Renewing the mind; brings soul into proper righteous position to express your spirit as it intuits the will of our Father! Without actively and progressively saving your soul, there remains an incongruity between spirit and soul. Your spirit hears from Holy Spirit; but your yet un-renewed mind causes constant buffeting and struggle to sabotage you carrying out the things of God! This mixture causes continuous stumbling and wavering in your daily walk! It is this mixture; this clash and struggle, that the Apostle Paul alludes to in Romans 7:14-15;18

for we know that the law is spiritual, but I am carnal, sold under sin. For that which I do I allow not; for what I would, that do I not; but what I hate, that do I.

[vs 18] for I know that in me (that is, in my flesh) dwelleth no good thing; for to will is present with me, but how to perform that which is good I find not; [vs19] for the good that I would, I do not: but the evil which I would not, that I do. [vs 21] I find then a law that when I would do good, evil is present with me.

This is the struggle of soul against spirit in the renewing of the mind. This is where the Word of God, steadily applied; begins to demolish the strongholds of the mind. The soul starts to become gradually converted; and then transformed; and eventually there is this beautiful congruence of spirit and soul. Your Father graces you with the will to do it!

Wherefore, lay apart all filthiness and superfluity of naughtiness, and receive with meekness the engrafted Word, which is able to save your soul." James 1:21

This responsibility to "save your soul" is given to us; according to the pleasure of God's will. It is to your honor that you co-labor with God to do so for we are in covenant with God; and covenant takes two! Since the Church have basically ignored this great honorable mandate; we've perish needlessly; and become victims as we cast blame on a weakened defeated foe. We have been sleepwalking on the admonitions of God's Word.

For we are laborers together with God; ye are God's husbandry; ye are God's building. 1Cor.3:9

Co laboring with the Father is actually a part of our covenant responsibility; given to us by our Father; and it is mandatory! It is not: maybe you can work with God to save your soul; rather it is a beautiful, soft, gentle commandment. God has done His part in this awesome covenant! He even makes you willing to work alongside Him in the saving of your soul! God is always intentional regarding His Kingdom purposes! He is building in us a temple; a building, an abode fit for His presence. We are to be about the business of building Him a house; which is us! We ought to be always working with the Father; always co-laboring with Him. *Isaiah.66:1 declares:*

Heaven is my throne, and the Earth is my footstool. Where is the house that ye build unto me and where is the place of my rest?

THE POWER OF THE WORD OF GOD.

Scriptures tells us to *be transformed by the renewing of your mind (Romans 12:2).* To re-iterate: Yahweh does His part and you are saved positionally. Nonetheless, experientially, you get to ratify your part of the covenant in re-aligning the mind/soul to the mind of

Christ; so that your soul might rightly reflect your spirit. Allowing Holy Spirit to take over your life causes you to be ruled by the spirit, and the decisions you make will be spiritual decisions. **The renewing of the mind is how you save your soul!**

Wherewithal shall a young man change his way? by taking heed thereto according to thy word. Thy word have I hid in mine heart, that I might not sin against thee (Ps.119: 9,11).

Is not my Word like a fire saith the Lord; and like a hammer that breaketh the rock in pieces (Jer.23:29).

When applied repeatedly, the Word effectively demolishes the strongholds of the mind. The Word of God is the will of God; and where the will of God is known, faith exists! Amen! Thus it is only through a renewed mind that you begin to understand the unfolding will of God. For only the Word of God has transforming power! It is expedient then, that the Word of God is applied to our lives daily. Gradual, consistent application of the Word causes you to grow and be strengthened in the grace of Jesus.

The kingdom of heaven is like unto leaven, which a woman took and hid in three measures of meal till the whole was leavened.

The Word of God is that [leavening] fermenting agent which causes a powerful multiplication of the light, knowledge and truth of God in your soul. It "leavens" or grows expeditiously within the soul, in increments until you experience "salvation" in that particular area as Scriptures says. As you begin to become filled up with the knowledge of God, you begin to grow from faith to faith (Roms.1:17); and move from strength to strength (Ps.84:7) and go from glory to glory (2Cor.3:18). Believers are called to walk in and apply the Word of God to our everyday lives; for your soul's saving!

receive with meekness the engrafted word which is able to save your soul (James 1:21.)

The Word of God supplies the information both about our Father; as well as about who He has made you and I to be. It is a beautiful loving responsibility that our Heavenly Daddy has bestowed upon us. Once you experience initial salvation and have been born again, there is a new learning that you need! It is learning about the One

Who saves you! Jesus say *"take my yoke upon you and learn of me (Matt.11:29), and we* rejoice in that we are saved by Jesus's blood! Amen! Once saved though, too many believers tend to then stand still, and wait to "be taken out of here" to heaven. Where we have erred through ignorance, is in not fulfilling our role as co-laborers with the Father! We are told in the Word:

when anyone hears the words of the kingdom and understandeth it not, then cometh the wicked one, and catcheth away that which was sown in his heart (Matthew 13:19).

The Word of the Kingdom is one of dominion! Man was created king and priest! To have rule; a demi-god; with power in his mouth; to co-create by the spoken word; to make and degree laws; and live above the beggarly things of this Earth. Made in the very image and after the likeness of His father Yahweh, man is given delegated authority. This is the word of the Kingdom! It is about Jesus Himself; and we are to be conformed to His image (Roms.8:27)! A lack of understanding of Who Yahweh is, and who you are: renders you as "dung for the fodder!"

The heart there is the soul/ mind; which is the very seat of your thoughts, passions, desires, appetites, affections, will and purposes! The Word of the Kingdom causes us to remember our dominion in Christ! When Adam fell on his head like Humpty Dumpty, all of mankind forgot the wonders of Who God is, and who we are in Him from the beginning! The devil fearfully and cunningly snatches it out of your mind/awareness, so that the carnal mind remains un-renewed, and thus continues to lead that soulish believer astray.

to be carnally-minded is death: but to be spiritually minded is life and peace Romans 8:6.

SAVING YOUR SOUL: A PRACTICAL APPLICATION.

It is very important that believers grasp that saving one's soul is a necessity; and an individual's responsibility to do so once you are born again; and over your entire lifetime! Believers struggle and stumble less and less once the mind is being renewed. Saving the soul gets your mind in alignment with spirit. Understanding the Word of the Kingdom is the understanding of the authority, the responsibility and trust which Yahweh entrusted to us. We are still required to "dress and keep" [the Garden]: the consciousness of Christ. Yet believers still pray for God to take their sins away, to deliver them, when Scriptures tells us that we are dead to sin but alive to Christ. We are admonished to "put off the old man... and put on the new man (Eph.4:22-24); yet believers pray to the Father every-day for Him to do it for us! The word of God causes our mind to both remember as well as know what God has done in Christ.

So beloved, you can say that you are believing for the healing of your back. Yet that same mouth of yours is used to dismantle the very thing that you say that you believe for, because all the time you are saying things like **my back is killing me or, I have a bad back.** In that you have just mixed the seed. For you show through your words that you believe less in your healing, and much more in what you are feeling! **Saving the soul is on purpose, intentionally, and methodically filling your mouth with what the word of God says concerning your healing;** not just praying for God to heal you! Your mind hears what your mouth speaks! **This is ordering your conversation; and as Scriptures say; you will see the salvation of God, whatever the situation (Ps. 50:24). Selah!**

Jesus answered the tempter with *It is written*! You will begin to renew your mind as you declare "it is written" to whatever situation that arises. This is how you cast down imaginations of the mind, and break stronghold of the flesh. You agree with God's word when you speak it; and the fermenting power of the word you speak causes transformation, as the power of the Word of God swallows up the darkness of the strongholds in your mind! By speaking what the word says concerning your healing; deliverance, finances, health, wealth, faith and all things pertaining to your life; and continue to do so; you build a stronghold of the Word in your spirit as well as your soul.

THE POWER OF THE RENEWED MIND

The intentional, constant declaration of the Word of God begins to become a lifestyle; as you walk daily with Holy Spirit! Man joined to the Lord is one spirit (1Cor.6:17); and the Holy Spirit enlightens you through your spirit, for your spirit is the candle of the Lord (Pro.20:27). The Word of God rightly applied to the soul of man, causes your mind to begin to re-align to its purposed position as it becomes transformed unto God's will. As strongholds of the mind crumble and fall; the soul again, as at creation, becomes the expression of spirit! Amen! As you need food for your natural body, so the Word of God is your soul's food! Soon the one thing coming from you lip, is the Word of God concerning any and every aspect of your life! At this juncture, through your wholesome tongue, the Word becomes a tree of life which in turn feeds your very soul! The Word beloved, is the Tree of life! At this point, you now know experientially, that your soul is undergoing transformation indeed!

Now we have received, not the spirit of the world, but the spirit which is of God; that we might know the things that are freely given to us of God. (1Cor.2:10-12)

The renewed mind grows in understanding, both of the glories of our Father Creator, as well as of who we were created to be. A renewed mind poses a dangerous threat to the kingdom of darkness, for authority is what satan desires! Once your mind has been renewed unto the Kingdom of God; satan cannot snatch the word from that heart! For such a paradigm recognizes the responsibility, honor, authority and stewardship one has been entrusted with, as a king on the Earth. That mindset humbly recognizes that the kingdom, the power, and the glory belongs to our Father! Amen!

Every scribe which has been instructed unto the kingdom of heaven is like unto a man that is a householder, which bringeth forth out of his treasure things new and old (Matt.13:52).

All thoughts, mindsets, concepts, and ideas, must be obliterated by the Word of God. It is your responsibility! The renewed mind follows hard after and is led by the Holy Spirit! Working out your salvation is the ultimate radical step of faith: *1Pet.1: 8-9 says:*

Whom having not seen, ye love; in whom, though now you see Him not, yet believing, ye rejoice with joy unspeakable and full of glory: Receiving the end of your faith, even the salvation of your soul. Amen and amen!

PART II

BACK TO WHERE IT ALL STARTED

CHAPTER 11

GOD'S ORIGINAL PLAN
OF SALVATION

As to His essence, God is Spirit. He is Love, and He is Light! Man,being created in the image of God, is a created spirit, and is a little god. Let's be clear here: dogs have puppies, cats have kittens and God created man as a god beneath Him, (Psalm 82:6). This is the very principle of a seed reproducing after its own kind (Genesis 1:11). **The word "god" means one empowered to rule.** Man was empowered by God to rule Earth while God the Father and Lord ruled the Heavens. Father then blessed man to *"be fruitful and multiply; to replenish the earth and subdue it(Gens.1:26-28):* Man thus have dominion on earth.

God created the heavens, the earth and all that are in them by His Word. The first Word God spoke was *"let there be light."* **Light is energy; so, the very first thing God did was to release of His Essence, His Energy into the Earth**. Since then, light has been moving at 186,000 miles per seconds. Man, created in the image and after the likeness of God, is also a creative, speaking spirit. Thus, whatever a man speak, comes to pass: for man was created from the very Energy /Word or sperma of his father Jehovah.

Being born again not of corruptible seed, but of incorruptible, by the word of God which liveth and abideth forever. 1 Peter 1:23

It is for this reason Jesus tells us that death and life is in the power of the tongue! (Pro.18:21). Jesus also declared that His words are both *spirit and life* (John 6:63); and since Jesus spoke only the Word of His Father; His words only create life. Man being joined to the Lord is one spirit (1Cor.6:17); as well as being joint heir with Jesus! Amen! **Man has an awesome responsibility to steward the fruit of his**

45

lips; just as Jesus did! For when you speak, you are actually creating realms; for your words have spirit or energy; and they move at the speed of light! Even though you might not immediately see the manifestation in the natural; in the realm of spirit; energy has already formed what you have spoken. This is the authority Man was given; and God put man's authority on display (see Chapter 8).

and whatsoever Adam called every living creature, that was the name thereof. Genesis.2:19

This is the first principle of delegated authority in action in the Bible. It shows the beauty of the Father's heart; that His son would have rulership in the realm of earth. This is the amazing, mind boggling privilege and beauty that we were endued with by our loving Creator. Furthermore, this move was a demonstration and a precept to man; of the power of the spoken word; as well as the responsibility, and stewardship which man was entrusted with, and therefore ought to exercise with that power. Man was now a small god and a ruler on earth; with power in his mouth. To this end Jesus declared to us:

you will have what you say (Mark 11:24).

Before there was creation there was the Word (John1:1). To live in this earth realm Jehovah wrapped man's spirit in a soul and gave him a body. The soul houses our mind, our will, our intellect, ego, personality, our memory, our imagination, our intuition and our emotions. Man's spirit was created to rule him as he receives from his Father; and be expressed through his soul as personality.

Jehovah planned to have man rule as kings on the earth while He, Jehovah, the Supreme King, would stay in Heaven. When His man Adam committed high treason, a curse was enforced, and man's mind became thwarted and corrupted. The light in man's spirit went out! The soul which should have been the expression of man's spirit, now assumed rule over man's spirit. Man's body which had been created to live free of sickness, was now subject to disease and all kind of maladies!

At regeneration (the work of Holy Spirit), the light in man's spirit which is the candle of the Lord (Proverbs 20:27) was re-lit or born again. The body which became diseases and corrupted, will be saved when corruption puts on incorruption (1 Cor.15:42-44; 52-54). The soul is that which is being saved in the lifetime of a man.

THE GODHEAD!

John 1:1 tells us: *"In the beginning was the Word, and the Word was with God and the Word was God."*

We can see the Father Who is God, the Son Jesus Who is and was the Word, and Holy Spirit Who was with God [just as you have your spirit with you always]. The Holy Spirit is both the Spirit of the Father and the Spirit of the Son, because the Father and the Son are One. Jesus confirmed this, declaring that *I and my Father are one* (*John 10:30*). When asked by Phillip to *show us the Father,* Jesus answered him saying *have I been with you this long and you have not known me, Phillip? (John 14:9)* This is irrefutable evidence of the Godhead—three personalities, distinct, but One! John tells us further:

For there are three which bear record in heaven, the Father, the Word, and the Holy Ghost: and these three are one.

And there are three that bear witness in earth, the Spirit, and the water and the blood and these three agree as one. (1 John 5:7-8).

Isaiah 9:6 prophesied: *unto us a child is born, unto us a son is given:.. and his Name shall be called Wonderful Counsellor, the* **Mighty God, the Everlasting Father**. Jesus is the *express image of the Father* (Hebrews 1:3). Jesus is God! Thus in Genesis at the dawn of creation when God spoke the heavens and earth into being, the Godhead was present. It was to this Trinity that God the Creator spoke; *"Let us make man."* Gens. 1:26).

The Father was present, the Son was present, and Holy Spirit was present; and the Holy Spirit took notes and wrote the Book. **The Godhead, distinct in personalities but One (Deut. 6:4) is the Father in Creation, the Son in redemption and Holy Spirit in regeneration. Amen!**

CHAPTER 12

KINGSHIP THROUGH SALVATION OR SALVATION THROUGH KINGSHIP?

F irstly, let's deal with the half-truth that Jesus came to Earth for our salvation. This is not an error, but it is certainly not the full oracle of God! Nowhere in Scripture are we told that Jesus came for our salvation. Jesus' accusers stated that He went about saying He was a king- not a savior. It was for this so called "blasphemy" that Jesus was crucified. Accused by His nation and asked of Pilate in (John 18:37): *Are you a king then?* Jesus answered, *"To this end was I born and for this cause came I into the world"*

Very, clearly stated! Jesus: in keeping with His Father's plan for an earthly Kingdom of kings, demonstrated authority as well as dominion during His short life on the Earth. At the Cross, we know that Jesus's body was mutilated; and we understand that as the blood ran down his entire body, our bodies were healed.

"Emancipate yourself from mental slavery" sings reggae artist Bob Marley in *Redemption Song*. This rings so true, for it is our own thinking that allows us to be devoured by the wiles of the enemy. The United Negro College Fund has a fabulous quote: "A mind is a terrible thing to waste." Profound and Biblical! Scriptures say we must renew our minds (Romans 12:2). Too often believers put total responsibility for our transformation onto God; not recognizing the power of our covenant, which involves two! God our loving Father mandated that we do our part to work with Him.

Yahweh's sovereign plan remains unchangeable; Man is to walk in and exercise both authority and dominion in the earth. Kings decree things and they are established. That's what kings do! Every time man went off track, Scriptures clearly show how God would reiterate man's purpose on the Earth. When God delivered ancient Israel out of Egyptian bondage, Jehovah reminded them that if they would keep His Covenant, they would be to Him:

a kingdom of priests in the earth (Exodus 19:4-6)

unto Him that loved us and washed us from our sins in His own blood, and hath made us kings and priests unto God… Rev.1:5.6

And hast made us unto our God, kings and priests: and we shall reign on the earth. Rev.5:10 declares.

Jesus came as a king, and all His teachings centered around the Kingdom of Heaven. He also mandated His disciples to declare the Kingdom of Heaven everywhere they preached. He bore the title of King of kings. Scriptures also give us a picture of how the end will look (1 Corinthians 15:24-28).

then cometh the end when He shall have delivered the kingdom to God, even the Father; when He shall have put down all rule and all authority and power.

Let us be clear: there is a Kingdom to be accessed now! Man was put on earth to be Father's representative: to multiply the awareness of the Christ; to co-labor with Jehovah to bring His will into the earth realm. **From this vantage point, man now becomes a power broker: endued with the amazing ability to stay here on the earth, yet be a broker of heavenly things. Thus, man brings Heaven into this realm; with the spoken word**; for king rule by declarations! Jesus promised that our heritage as believers is to:

see heaven open, and the angels of God ascending and descending upon the Son of man. John 1:51

Jesus is the means, the ladder between Heaven and Earth. We who are joint heirs with Jesus get to go up and down the ladder, bringing the Kingdom into our situation anytime and in any circumstances. Rather than open your mouth and agree with a deceitful, nasty foe, you ought always to agree with our Almighty God and Father; as did the Pattern Son! After He was resurrected, Jesus told Mary:

49

go to my brethren and say unto them, I ascend unto my Father and your Father; and to my God and your God! (John 20:17).

We are children of the King of Glory! Protocol mandates that we speak, act and behave in manners fitting of the King's sons! Amen! While we clearly understand that Jesus is our Savior; to think that He came only to save us from sins and for Heaven is not an error at all. Yet it is certainly not the full counsel of God! **A mindset which sees Jesus coming to earth to re-establish His Father's kingdom on Earth, and thus bringing regeneration to fallen mankind as a part of that journey, produces a kingdom paradigm.** The Jews of Jesus's time certainly expected a king who would have restored to Israel a kingdom; his disciples clearly said so in Acts 1:6. For then, mankind would be reunited and restored to the mission of establishing God's Kingdom in the Earth realm. There is a kingdom to be had!

WHERE IS satan IN ALL THIS?

First, we have preached salvation as the end all rather than as the beginning. As stated earlier, that doesn't make it an error. However, it represents only a thirty- fold revelation of the Kingdom! **That is a mindset from which we must evolve, in order to see the bigger picture and rise up to be the kings we were created to be.** Adam's treason was no surprise to an all-knowing God and Father. Adam had to fail so God would have legal entry into the earth realm. Mankind was made subject to vanity by His Father (Roms. 8:19-20); so that the mature sons of God would eventually come forth and liberate the creation.

Adam's sin made way for Jesus the God man to become the son of man; to restore God's intent. Adam, the man, lost his kingship to satan, and a man named Jesus came and got it back by "whupping" satan. Much like a bully (satan) beating up on a kid, taking away his daddy's stuff: Jesus our senior brother came and thrashed the bully and got his Daddy's stuff back.

The first man Adam was made a living soul; the last Adam was made a quickening spirit. (1 Cor. 15:45-49)

Jesus, the Lamb, had been slain from the foundation of the earth (Revelation 13:8). **Jesus' crucifixion on Calvary's Cross, was a**

physical show of what had already occurred before time; so that man could visually see the plan of God. Calvary's cross, as a symbolic metaphor, is the act of appeasement necessary to wipe out our sinful nature as well as our sin consciousness. We see Jesus as a sacrifice: a propitiation for sin as the Scripture declares. (1John 2:2.) Dictionarysearch.com states propitiation is "a conciliatory offering to a god."

Men died on the cross before and after Jesus, let's be clear about that. **It is symbolic of Jesus our Savior King nailing our sins to the Cross.** In the resurrection, Jesus both dealt with the restoration of intimacy with our Father, as well as with recovering and restoring to man: the glory, authority and power, victory and dominion he had been given.Man was also delegated the keys of the Kingdom of God the Father. Jehovah relaxed and watched, because before time was, the Father, the Son and Holy Spirit had the conversation and the covenant was cut! It was well planned, and it was a done deal!

Second, our salvation is not a battle to get to heaven. The buffeting of the carnal mind against the mind of Christ is constant. Yet the level of buffeting decreases to the degree that one renews the mind. There is no constant need to fight against satan as so many in the Church have preached. **It is perverse to think that the Church has been clamoring to get to Heaven as if our Heavenly Daddy made it a task for us.** We believers live in the earth which is ruled by the evil negativity of the kingdom of darkness rules! As citizens of the Kingdom of Heaven we realize the constant buffeting from the inferior kingdom. Yet it is never a fight; Jesus has already won and we have been made more than conquerors. (Rom.8:31-39). Yet we do wrestle!

The only fight the believer has is that *fight of faith as 1 Tim. 6:12 says.* This entails standing on the Word of Almighty God, declaring it, and laying hold of what He says, by faith; and then resting in His promises. **The lack of faith is the** *sin which doth so easily beset us (Heb.12:1).* Being here on earth surrounded by, and being buffeted constantly by the kingdom of darkness; and at times looking with our natural eyes, too often we believe the things we see. Jesus came declaring:

Repent: for the kingdom of heaven is at hand. (Matthew 4:17).

Jesus never once said your salvation is at hand. The Kingdom is the destination; salvation is a consequence of the kingdom. The fight of faith is a good fight; and we engage in knowing that Jehovah;

hasten my[His] words to perform them (Jer.1:12);

He magnifies His words above His Name (Ps.138:2);

His word is "settled in heaven" (Ps.119:89). Selah!

The shedding of blood cleansed both the heavens and the Earth, and remitted man's sinful nature. Our salvation is necessary to realign our intimate fellowship with our loving Heavenly Daddy. It is a love walk with our Father, and Jesus is the Father's love gift to mankind! As we walk together, we wield a two- edged sword in our hands (Ps.149:6), in authority; subduing the Earth; and bringing Jehovah's will from Heaven to the Earth realm.

While we enter the Kingdom through much tribulation; Jesus admonished us to be of good courage because He has already overcome (John 16:33)! We must put away the negative mindset of everything being hard and difficult when Jesus has already told us that His yoke is easy and His burden is light (Matthew 11:30). So even in tribulation; you get to access the kingdom; and experience the joy which results from living in God's Kingdom.

Here on earth, we can have "heaven on earth" if we follow His precepts and keep His laws. Satan is nowhere in this! The Kingdom of Heaven is about the King and His sons! In the Kingdom of God, the Lamb is the Light and there is no night there; for the Christ nature of the overcomer cast out the serpent.Rev.22:5. Selah

SPIRITUAL DOWNLOADS

Think about modern technology as an analogy of our fellowship with Jehovah. We are a kind of prototype in the Earth, [peculiar, royal priesthood], and Yahweh our master Brain/Mind lives in heaven.We receive constant "downloads" from our Heavenly Daddy by way of e-mail, messages and attachments. We can talk to Him anytime in a gibberish-like language [tongues], which cannot be intercepted or understood by our arch enemy! There are times when we receive instruction via "webinars" and always through messages, whether via texts or e-mails. We are aware of the dark lord who "spams us" with unsolicited e-mail, promises, and deceptive lies and sends us malware and vicious viruses to corrode and render our operating systems inoperative. Believers shouldn't even bother open his spam mail at all, for we are not ignorant of his devices.

Casting down imaginations and every high thing that exalteth itself against the knowledge of God. And bringing into captivity every thought to the obedience of Christ; And having in a readiness to revenge all disobedience (2 Cor. 10:5-6).

That means the images- of- nations in your mind! They only exist there because the serpent gets to eat the dust of our fallen mind. **The knowledge of God are the things concerning what Christ did and what Christ says concerning His and our Father: anything else is a "high thing!"** Remember we perish because of a lack of knowledge. Never let it be from such things which come from your mouth! The utmost important thing is increasingly getting more of the knowledge of God! Only the Word supplies that, so we align our mouths with the Word of God. Once you are equipped with the Word in your heart; and live by it; your way is illuminated! Psalms 119:105 declares:

Thy Word is a lamp unto my feet and a light unto my path

A renewed mind doesn't succumb to the wiles of the enemy. satan can only go about as *a roaring lion, seeking whom he may devour.* (1Pet.5:8). The "whom" are those with un-renewed minds concerning the 'purpose and knowledge of Almighty God. The Word of God, being appropriated daily is the antidote! **Kingdom teaching and preaching brings a powerful new paradigm which keeps the evil one where he belongs; under our feet! Salvation through the Kingdom gives a fresh perspective of Whose we are and of who we are! Amen!**

And the God of peace shall wound satan under your feet shortly. The grace of our Lord Jesus Christ be with you. Romans 16:20. Amen!

Thy kingdom come, thy will be done, on earth as it is in heaven. Amen! Selah!

CHAPTER 13

GOD OR SATAN?

C learly satan and Jehovah are not in the same league. Jehovah is the Creator, and satan is a created being: a type of Darth Vader, the dark lord who seeks always to destroy the kingdom. Matter of fact, it was Jehovah's idea to subject His own creation to this corruption, for His hope was to raise up for Himself a new breed. Jehovah placed His trust in man; that in time His sons would become liberators and mature rulers of this new realm. Even now, the whole of creation is in ordeal: a kind of labor pain: waiting for the mature sons of Yahweh to arise and liberate them from evil corruption. (Romans 8:18-20-22).

It is little wonder that we love superheroes, for inert within all of mankind's spirit is a taste of eternity that was placed there by the Father (Ecc.3:11). We are all of us; a kind of hero! So, we long to be great, to help our fellowman, and to shine a light for others! We desire to live epic lives: that we might live above the beggarly elements of the world; for we all want to rule and be successful. We were created that way! Yet because of ignorance we languish daily, becoming watchers of other men's passion; dreaming of being great ourselves—all the time not realizing that the hero lies within. The Kingdom of God is within us! We—all of mankind— were created kings unto our Eternal God and Father. However when we do not rule in a manner fitting for kings, we ourselves become enslaved.

WHAT OF SICKNESS?

Jesus told us over and over that He was one with His Father (John14:9-11; 17:21). Scripture reiterates this Oneness many times! (Deut. 6:4;1 John5:7-8; Heb.1:3,8). Jesus the Son always did the will of the Father (John 5:19). **The Godhead doesn't work against itself; they are One! So, no! Jesus didn't die for our sickness and disease, in order for the Father to turn around and put sickness on His creation to teach us lessons. That is a perverted belief—a thief that has robbed us from the glory of the Father's love; and left the Church schizoid and weak.** As a part of the kingdom paradigm coming to the earth, Jesus instructed His disciples to:

Heal the sick, cleanse the lepers, raise the dead, cast out devils" (Matthew 10:7-8; Mark 16:17-18).

Sickness is neither good nor is it prosperous, and to think that sickness would be a part of Father's expected end is just plain perverse. For our loving heavenly Father tells us in Jeremiah 29:11:

For I know the thoughts that I think towards you, saith the LORD, thoughts of peace, and not of evil, to give you an expected end.

Notwithstanding, once sickness is present, Father can and often works through sickness and wraps His purpose around it, but to say post-Calvary, that God put sickness on us to teach us a lesson, is both warped and disturbing. A PERVERTED BELIEF!

To believe that God, Creator; Who is Love, would do that to his own creation, while you yourself wouldn't think to do that to your own children, is both wicked and is pure heresy! If you feel like God punishes His children with sickness, to humble them; the next time your child misbehaves, I guess you could go ahead and pray sickness on that child, to punish her. Then feel how dirty and defiled you feel! Why then do you give medicine to your children? Or take any medicine for yourself; if you believe that God wants you sick, and punishes you with sickness?! Don't you want to be like God?

If you find it an evil thing to withhold good from your children; yet believe that God, our Father does that to us His children; you would essentially be saying that you are more loving than God! That kind of perverse thinking stems from a lack of understanding the Father Heart of God. He is not just God- He is Father! Our Father, and it is the manner of love He has for us that makes us sons (1John 3). We are sons through Father's love: Jesus came to make us family! So to think that Daddy sent His Son to bring us back to Himself, to heal and deliver us, only to turn around and afflict us with evil in the form of sickness and disease: is a schizoid, wicked, adulterous and utterly perverted, warped, image of God!

If ye then being evil, know how to give good gifts unto your children; how much more shall your Father which is in heaven, give good things to them which ask Him (Matthew 7:11)

If you really do believe that; then not only do you **not trust** the Lord; but you cannot be truly intimate with Him; for there is no intimacy with any person you cannot trust. That no doubt affects your relationship with the Lover of your soul! It shows a searing lack of, and ignorance of the knowledge of the Father. Your lack of knowledge of the oracles of Yahweh is causing you to perish, and to be fodder for the devil. That kind of reasoning is carnal; and is meat for the enemy. It is an **ungodly leaven of the soul;** it will cause you to live beneath the blessings and beauty of being a son of the Father.

For my thoughts are not your thoughts, neither are your ways my ways saith the Lord. (Isaiah 55:8)

The Word of God is the one thing that our Creator has esteemed above His very name (Psalm 138:2). I urge you to prayerfully search the Scriptures; and cry out for understanding as you diligently seek after the knowledge of Yahweh! You must believe what Scriptures says; and believe in the Father Who wrote this book of Love letters to His children. Then, hunger and thirst to experience the fiery love of the Father! It will totally transform you! You will grow in knowledge of God; and you will be able to prove what the will of God is (Romans 12:2). I promise you, that the Word of God will totally transform your life as you begin to encounter the Father's love; and it will prevent you from being destroyed.

That ye, being rooted and grounded in love, may be able to comprehend with all the saints, what is the breadth, and length, and depth, and height; and to know the love of Christ, which passeth all knowledge, that ye may be filled with all the fulness of God!

PART III

OUR POWER AND AUTHORITY

CHAPTER 14

THE PATH OF TRUE POWER

I n Genesis 2:19 **God brought all the creatures to Adam "to see" what Adam would name them.** This demonstrates a very beautiful principle of delegated authority shown through divine trust! It also sets the precedence for the entire Bible as well as for the entire race called mankind.

Mankind: this specie was created a race of kings and priests unto God, on the Earth, exercising authority and dominion. Kings are born kings; not made: and by virtue of the title, kings make decrees. A king's authority is always demonstrated when he speaks; his words hold much sway! This is an aspect of the mystery the Apostle Paul mentions repeatedly in his letters to the Church of his day.

How that by revelation he made known unto me the mystery; (as I wrote afore in few words), whereby, when ye read, ye may understand my knowledge in Christ

Which in other ages was not made known unto the sons of men, as it is now revealed unto His holy apostles and prophets by the Spirit: that the Gentiles should be fellow heirs, and of the same body, and partakers of his promise in Christ by the gospel. (Eph.3:3-4;9).

The enemy first had Adam and Eve to ignore and question the knowledge of Who God their Father is; and the knowledge of who God had created them to be. They did; thus betraying the Empire through high treason! The devil began to understand even more, that the power lies in the mouth of kings speaking the Word of Yahweh. When Adam sinned in the midst of a perfect garden; **satan thought he had won; but he never recognized Jesus as the last Adam; and the second man! satan totally never understood the power of the resurrection!** satan realized his mistake too late; for in an instant: he was totally stripped of his power and authority, with no hope of ever again, getting back what that he had stolen from Adam! *1Cor.15:21, 45-47 declares:*

For since by man came death, by man came also the resurrection of the dead. For as in Adam all die, even so in Christ shall all be made alive.

And so it is written, the first man Adam was made a living soul: the last Adam was made a quickening spirit

The first man is of the earth, earthy: the second man is the Lord from heaven!

The devil does and will always operate as he did with Adam and Eve, and as he unashamedly repeated with Jesus the only begotten Son of God. In His temptation, Jesus left us with the Pattern of how we ought to operate when assaulted by the devil. Jesus did not react, as believers often become; and Jesus did not start a fight with the enemy; but He did respond all three times with:

It is written! (Luke 4:4-14; Matt.4:4-10).

By attempting to thwart the knowledge of God in our eyes satan still doesn't yet understand the wisdom of God! For, just as Jehovah entrusted His first man; Father totally trusts Jesus His Son! Now through His Son; comes the Church: that many- membered Body of Christ! The Church through the power of Jesus is the last instrument being used by the Father to usher in His Kingdom here on the earth. **Post Calvary; we do not have to fight with the enemy! Jesus has already won the victory!** Jesus has also made us more than conquerors through His shed blood (Rom.8:34-37). What we the Church get to do as kings and priests: is respond with the Word of God, just as Jesus did! Jesus is always the Pattern! Amen!

The Word of God is food and sustenance for us as citizens of the Kingdom of Heaven. We ought to live by and speak only the Word of God! We believe in and speak about: who God says He is; His testimony, and of His commandment; His fear; His statues and His judgements! The Oracles of Almighty God; Who is our Abba- [Daddy] Father; is what we speak!! What an awesome privilege! This is the path of true power! Psalms 19:7 declares:

The law of the Lord is perfect, converting the soul.

Father God loves to showcase His might and power! When He delivered ancient Israel out from the Egyptian bondage; He did so with great might and powerful displays of His wonder and power! In these end times; God's intent is that the Seed of Abraham, numerous as the sand on the shore; would wield His power and authority; through our spoken word and lifestyle!

The great Mind and Intelligence of God our Father, is to yet use the Church: an extensive company of men and women, great and small: from every tribe, nation and tongue, **to showcase Himself: that He is Lord of the whole Earth!** Amen! His intent has not changed! Daddy wants us, the Church: male and female both, mighty super-heroes and deliverers, to stun the dark kingdom of satan, while they watch in amazement; as did Pharaoh and his company! *Ephesians 3:9,10 says*

And to make all men see what is the fellowship of the mystery, which from the beginning of the world hath been hid in God, Who created all things by Jesus Christ: ***To the intent that now unto the principalities and powers in heavenly places, might be made known by the Church, the manifold wisdom of God.***

For the earth shall be filled with the knowledge of the glory of the Lord, as the waters covers the seas. (Habakkuk 2:14)

But as truly as I live, all the earth shall be filled with the glory of the Lord. Numbers 14:21

The path of true power lies in your ability to receive and understand the beauty and simplicity of Who Yahweh is; through His Son Jesus. **As a nation, Israel knew the acts of God; and Moses knew His ways! We are called to know the very Person of God!** Old mindsets, sacred cows and Perverted Beliefs within the Church at large, have led many away captives; dull of hearing and forgetful! Jesus came to set the captives free! As an ambassador of the Kingdom, you **re-present** God! As a son; understanding your kingship is to be manifested in your language! **Your responsibility is to steward your words with intention: and bring the reality of the Kingdom of Heaven to every sphere of earth!** Amen!

CHAPTER 15

A PARADIGM SHIFT

aradigm refers to a set of ideology, beliefs, mindsets and concepts that we hold to. We are believers because we BELIEVE the Word of God. When we agree with wrong mindsets; thinking and imaginations; we come into agreement with the enemy; and the devil uses those to steal our God-given passions and desires, kill our dreams and aspirations and destroy our purpose; which is to be conformed to the image of His Son (Romans 8:29). In order for us to destroy strongholds in our thinking; we must re-align our minds with the mind of Christ! **We need a shift in our thinking for we were all blinded and suffered amnesia in the Fall of Man; and now we need to remember!**

And He took the blind man by the hand and led him out of the town; and when He had spit on His eyes, and put His hands upon him, he asked him if he saw ought. And he looked up, and said, I see men as trees, walking. After that again he put his hands again upon his eyes and made him look up: and he was restored and saw every man clearly. (Mark 8:22-25)

Jesus lovingly took the blind man by the hand and led him out of the town! **Town here is that collective mindset, ideology, beliefs, concepts and views of many people—what people said and were saying.** Jesus takes this blind man away from all that was familiar to him—what he was raised to believe; his culture and his current thinking and beliefs. Next Jesus put spit on his eyes: Jesus had to put His breath, His Word, His flavor, on the blind man's eye; for the eyes are the lens through which one sees. It was also like a kiss of heaven{Jesus) and earth; the blind man/mankind; much in the same manner that Father had breathed into Adam's nostrils in the beginning! Praise Yahweh!

Jesus then put his hands on him and asked him if he saw anything. The blind man's reply of, "I see men as trees, walking," was obviously not present physical reality! This blind man experienced a trip back into his origin; for in Adam, all of mankind was formed from the ground: just as were the trees (Gens.1:9-12; 2:7)! To the natural eye though, men are not as trees walking; but try telling a blind man who can only see in the spirit that truth! That was his perception though! Your reality as well, becomes shaped by your perception; whether thwarted or not! **When we are not beholding Yahweh as He is; we too are incidentally somewhat " blind" and in need of a second touch as did the blind man.**

Beloved, when that man first started to see; Jesus did not rebuke him at all! He was seeing something! No doubt, that man probably realized that he was in the presence of the One Who created his eyes to see in the first place! Hallelujah! Too often, the Church can be quick to rebuke and count out others who do not see as we do! **Jesus's second touch is a pattern and a model of how all of mankind's perception needs to be healed.** As believers, and as the Church collectively; we are admonished to be transformed through getting our mind renewed. This is also a model for us, for how we ought to walk others through the ministry of reconciliation.

A person's paradigm or belief system become formed from life experiences; what was said around you as you were growing up; by what popular media preaches, or by life's traumas and tragedies. You are a sum total of every person who has ever touched your life; for good or bad: especially your earliest caregivers. This is how we form image-nations [imaginations] in the mind. **Images which more than often, DO exalt themselves against the knowledge of Christ!** A paradigm shift is a radical change in how a person think views, and sees things. It is dramatic, sharp and powerful! Mankind even the Church, need a different paradigm of our Heavenly Father. Your perception forms your reality; even though your reality is not often based upon practical truth; as we see with this blind man.

All of us are in need of a second touch; we have all been "blind," having been born again out of a sin nature and in need of transformation of our mindset. Many people say that Scriptures should be left up to one's interpretation. **That is obviously perverse thinking, and it a great example of the soul ruling the spirit of a person!** That is carnal at its core, and will no doubt entertain beelzebub! It is dangerous! The mindset that the Almighty Creator and God would leave His Holy Word to the mind of his creation, having subjected man to fall at every level, **is both ridiculous and perverse!** It is fashioning God after the image of man; and based on the thoughts of fallen men. We must no longer ignore these things; but understand; and continue to search out the truth of the unfolding knowledge of Yahweh and His kingdom!

Scriptures must be interpreted based upon principles of the Bible, and purely from what the Word says. Oftentimes the issue arises as we attempt to understand and interpret the Bible—an eastern book—with a western mindset. Thus, if that is left to an individual's interpretation we would be in trouble! We saw that in Adam's and Noah's generations. For we interpret the Word of Scriptures based upon our belief systems and culture, even if they are rooted in superstition, utter nonsense and error, or just chop logic. For in so doing, **we sin as we fashion God after our soul's preference.** The soul always desires to rule as in the fall. The soul will always fashion a god who would bow to us. Our God bows to no man! He is the ALMIGHTY GOD and FATHER!

knowing this first, that no prophecy of the scripture is of any private interpretation, for the prophecy came not in old time by the will of man: but holy men of God spake as they were moved by the Holy Ghost (2 Peter 1:20, 21).

Another perverse belief some believers say at times; is that the Bible contradicts itself! Although this stems from ignorance on the part of a believer, it is a cunning trick of the enemy to criticize the Mind and Intelligence of God! It is a rather perverse view and impression of our Father and Creator! That the Almighty God and Creator; who knows all things; and the secrets of men's hearts; **would be so negligent, that He would write us a love manual which contradict itself! To lie to His children? Now that is truly vile and perverse and ought to be repented of!** My question to you would be; do you believe that you were given dominion; to rule as a king in the earth? Scripture declares:

Unto Him that loved us, and washed us from our sins in his own blood, and hath made us kings and priests unto God and His Father; to Him be glory, and dominion for ever and ever. Amen. Rev.1:5-6.

The Sovereign, all Wise, all Knowing God, Creator, and Father; in His Infinite Wisdom; subjected His own creation to fail. His hope was that of having a nation of kings and priest populating Earth; and through His Son, they would establish His Kingdom in the end (Roms.8:20)! Just as the infant Jesus was wrapped in swaddling clothes; God wrapped His Intention/ Purpose in two Covenants! Amen! His Word is loaded with mystery and hidden wisdom: kingdom oracles; precepts and principle! To His own glory, Amen! For God alone is the Supreme God! He hides things then He invites us His sons and daughters, to search out the hidden manna of His Word. Do you know that you are born a king?

It is the glory of God to conceal a thing: but the honor of kings is to search out a matter! (Proverbs 25:2)

The blind man experienced a radical shift in his thinking; and he saw men differently than he did before. So regardless of where you are; as you are willing to lay aside your beliefs, and like the blind man, allow Jesus; through His Word; to lovingly take you by the hand and walk you out of the "town," [old mindsets] and touch your eyes! Christ's mind is available for you!

Father, like that blind man, we cry out for a second touch; from the Second Man; that we might see with fresh eyes the beauty of Who you are. We lay aside and repent of the idols of our mind; our Perverted Beliefs which have kept us in bondage, and we receive freedom as we submit our will to Yours, Father, in Jesus Name. Amen!

CHAPTER 16

EVERY IDLE WORD

J esus preached the Kingdom of Heaven, healed the sick and cast out demons everywhere He went. On one occasion, in Matthew 12:22-31; after casting out a devil that had made one man both blind and dumb, the religious leaders accused Jesus of using beelzebub, the prince of devils, to cast the devils out. To use a devil to cast out another devil? How perverse is that?! Now, imagine with me; any kind of religious thinking that would support what those Pharisees thought about the matter! Can you see how one's belief can be the thief that would steal, kill and destroy one's liberty in Christ?

Jesus addressed that religious mindset! He told them they had an evil heart from which they spoke evil, corrupt things. This is a startling example of how perverse we can get—even the religious— in the name of God. **Yet how many times have members of the Body of Christ criticized healers who cast out devils and healed the sick?** To you now reading this book: Have you ever thought or questioned a healing or deliverance in disbelief? Have you said; or do you believe that healings, and miracles have passed away? Maybe you believe there are no real prophets or apostles today, even though Scriptures tell us that prophets and apostles are two of the five-fold ministry within the Body at large? (Ephesians 4:11).

There is no question of how perverse the Church has become, what with different denominations and varying belief systems! Some say speaking in tongues has passed away, some say it is still relevant to every believer, and others say it is of the devil. The beat goes on! Jesus addressed this manner of thinking and speaking:

That every idle word that men shall speak, they shall give account thereof in the day of judgment. For by thy words thou shall be justified and by thy word thou shalt be condemned. (Mat.12:36 – 37)

That there is just as clear as it gets! **Our words move us into righteousness or into condemnation.** There is no mention of our wicked adversary condemning us. So, let us unpack this great truth, for if we as His son kings do not search out a matter, we dishonor our Father; and our inaction becomes a thief and a robber.

It is the glory of God to conceal a thing: but the honor of kings is to search out a matter (Pro.25:2).

In the beginning of this Book, I stated that Christians will not face a condemnatory day of judgement; for we have passed from condemnation unto life. (John.5:24). Incidentally, for the most part; this Scripture concerning the "day of judgement" has been preached by most in the Church as a futuristic judgement day experience; and have thus missed a great key truth of God's word. Truth is layered so the full counsel of God might be revealed. Rather then, let us look at the same Scripture in the realm of now; for the Kingdom of Heaven is now! It is a present day reality. Look at this paradigm…

every negatively energized {useless, barren) word that a man speak, will create a [judgement] crisis for him; because by a man's word he shall be justified and by a man's word he shall be condemned. Matthew 12:36-37

Looking at **judgment only as "that day," we have missed very powerful and essentials keys to living in the Kingdom of Heaven right now, as well as prospering in the image of God in our daily lives!** What awesome responsibility we have been given to steward your word and thus create possibilities; in your own life as well as in the lives of others, as our Father intended! For Yahweh did give us authority in our mouths, as this writing has reiterated! Negative words, then, are perverse in God's mind; damaging to one's soul; and we are warned against uttering any kind of perversity from our lips (Proverbs 4:24).

Can you see that by looking only into the future, we have lost the prophetic power of now? The above Scripture holds believers **both accountable and responsible for shaping our lives by the words which come out of our mouths, today!** satan has neither the authority nor the power to condemn us! It doesn't even say that God will condemn us! It does show that **you have power to condemn yourself though: by your words**! That is quite sobering! Yahweh is altogether lovely! What an honor and an exceedingly great privilege to be able to speak and help shape your destination. That destination I am speaking of is being conformed to Christ's image!

For whom He did foreknow, He also did predestinate to be conformed to the image of His Son, that He might be the firstborn among many brethren. Romans: 8:29

CLEANING UP OUR MOUTHS

Coupled with the admonition of "idle words" we are also told *"Death and life are in the power of the tongue."* (Proverbs 18:21) So it is worth saying again that **your tongue has the power to create your reality**—that of death, decadence, ill health, sickness and disease, trouble, crisis, and all things dark. That kind of speaking provides "wood" which builds up the kingdom of darkness. And your tongue also has the power to create life—health, wealth, goodness, prosperity, peace and all things positive for you; as you agree with the Kingdom of Heaven! Then the responsibility rests squarely on your shoulders! **This is sound kingdom doctrine; and to deviate is contrary to God's Word, and is thus perverse!**

Can you see how, as small gods on the earth (Psalm 82:6), when we speak anything contrary to what God says or does; it is utterly perverse to the Lord, and the enemy uses that to build strongholds? As with Adam, **God brings things to you to see what you will call it;** and God does watch over His Word to perform it (Jer.1:12)! Now if God watches over His Word, it behooves us to watch over our words! For when our words do not align with the Word of God, there will be no involvement of His Deity! Amen.

Essentially, as Yahweh's royal ambassadors, we must always **be "re-presenting"** God to a dark and decaying world. Thus when life brings us the negatives, and when there is void/ barrenness as in the beginning, we ought imitate our Father; and speak light into dark situations. **Thus, we are creating new realms, new possibilities,** and delivering others from the evil! Light always causes darkness to flee. We are called by Jesus "the light of the world" and collectively;

we become that "city that is set on a hill" (Matt.5:14).

The Church, it behooves us to repent and begin to clean up our collective mouth; stop with the fascination with the devil that we have shown by our much devil speaking! We ought to be demonstrate the Mind and Intelligence of our Father, in a manner that stupefy satan's kingdom! (Eph.3:10)! Yahweh is and has always been intentional; and so, ought we! As believers individually, and collectively as the Church: as kings and sons who know that we have been given this awesome privilege and responsibility. Yahweh our Father is waiting, and watching.

It is noteworthy to mention that anything concerning satan dwells in the realm of darkness, negativity, decadence and death. Our work here is to **seek ye first the kingdom.** That will stop you from "looking" at satan-even in blame! Blame flows from a position of weakness, and it is eating from the tree of the knowledge of good and evil. That is what Adam and Eve did at the Fall. Let us look at the Christ, the Tree of Life instead, in praise and thanksgiving! We have been a perverse generation, so yes, we have been creating our own crises, every day, by the words we have been speaking.

and they who like it shall eat the fruit thereof. Proverbs 18:21

Jesus answered the temptations of the enemy with "It is written." His Body, must always do the same! We answer only with what the Bible says about the knowledge of God: not what the enemy is doing!This is kingdom talk; and kingdom thinking! Amen. Beloved, the negative fruit that has been manifesting in the Church results a lot from the Church energizing the enemy with much speaking. We know our adversary exists to buffet us constantly and he wants our demise! But from the beginning, our Father exercised His own faith in us His sons. This Ephesians 1:18 calls: *the hope of His calling.*

Because of the awesome power, authority and trust given to you as a son, every time you speak of satan and blame him for what is your role; you create a realm of possibility which gives him energy to operate—because you are a speaking spirit. Can you see how that puts the responsibility solely on you, and not on the devil? Since, this is **contrary to the Word of God, and because as "light" your word has energy, it is a psychic "soul" power which energies the** devil. Teaching about him, rebuking him, exposing and binding his works through the Word of God, is what you ought to be doing: as did Jesus! Strengthening him with the energy of the fruit of your mouth is perverse! Like your Father, your word is energy in motion!

Seriously, the Kingdom of Heaven is about a King and his sons: kings and priests walking in fellowship and bringing Heaven to Earth. We know there is a real devil, but in the Kingdom of God there is no serpent; **for the power of the nature of Christ within overcomes the devil; and he is cast out!** I understand some might say that the accuser appears before the throne of God and accuses the saints days and night. Yes, he did! However, I might also add that satan's access has been cut off through the finished work of Jesus. He has long been cast down to the earth and he occupies the heavens directly above us here on earth. Truth be told, we sit above him, positionally, in the Kingdom of God. *Ephesians 1:20-23 states*

which he wrought in Christ, when He raised Him from the dead and set Him at His own right hand in the heavenly places, far above all principality and power, and might, and dominion, and every name that is named, not only in this world, but also in that which is to come. And hath put all things under His feet, and gave Him to be head over all things to the Church, which is His body, the fulness of Him that filleth all in all.

The Prince of Persia is no longer holding up the answers to your prayers! Bless Jesus! Unless you live in Persia! This oft-mentioned prince was the ruling spirit over the geographical region where Daniel lived. Yes, there are principalities which exist over specific geographical regions above us, where you and I live. Different princes operate differently over different regions! In the **economy of the Kingdom of Heaven, we are seated above all principality and power!** We therefore have no need to **"get a prayer through"** for **the kingdom is within you (Lk.17:20-21).** satan is *the prince of the power of the air* (Ephesians 2:2): but it is believers who can now come boldly to the Throne of God and *obtain mercy and find grace to help in time of need* (Heb. 4:16).

The role of the local Church in any region is to identify the princes over that region, and cast them out; and then occupy the gates to that city! Bless Jesus! Yes, they are there opposing believers all the time. It is this **wrestling** *against principalities and powers* that is referenced in Ephesians 6:12; like two sumo wrestlers jockeying for position! The awesome thing is that the Kingdom of God has already won through Christ; and we sit together with Christ in heavenly places! (Eph.2:6). This also is indeed glorious!

satan has no real power! Did he ever hold power? Sure, for Adam gave up his power to the enemy; and the devil reminded Jesus of that fact (Matthew 4:9). However, at redemption, Jesus recovered the keys to hell and the grave and declared in Matthew 28:18!

all power in heaven and earth has been given to me.

That "all" power has been delegated to us by Jesus. What satan is afraid of is us knowing the **authority** we have in Christ because what satan wants is **power.** he now works relentlessly to steal our liberty in Christ! As when Adam blamed Eve, and she blamed the serpent; every time we place blame on a defeated devil, not only are we partaking of the tree of the knowledge of good and evil, as they did; but we would be invalidating the finished work of the Cross. Blame places us in a place of weakness; when we are told to be strong in the Lord and in the power of His might (Eph.6:10)!

What satan has, is wiles: deceit, trickery, vile, crafty and cunning ways of operating. **He works to sabotage your power: and this he does by the power of agreement! This is that physic, carnal ability of the carnal mind;** having believer to be led by the un-renewed soul instead of being spirit led, as he did with Adam and Eve. Anytime soul rules over spirit; the carnal mind is in control, and it gives the devil a physic kind of energized "power" to operate on (see Chapter 10)! The real power lies in the Kingdom of Heaven!

What we think and believe about satan is the issue—and one of the real thieves of John 10. If you believe that he has power, then you have already agreed that he will use it against you. That kind of belief means that you are already being led by your carnal mind, and that is his domain. That kind of thinking is in complete opposition to, and at enmity with God (Roms.8:6-7).

For thine is the kingdom, and the power, and the glory forever.

CHAPTER 17

WHAT IS THE
ARMOR OF GOD?

As dwellers on the Earth, with the inferior kingdom of darkness as the "ruling power" we believers need to be armored; fully armored the Bible says! As a defeated foe (1John3:8); the devil works relentlessly against us. There is and will be, constant buffeting; for the enemy does not let up: always he seeks any opening in which he can get a foothold. Our Father mandated us to be armored always for this reason.

*Finally, my brethren, be strong in the Lord, and in the power of His might. Put on the whole armor of God, that ye might be able to stand against the wiles of the devil. For we wrestle not against flesh and blood, but against principalities, against powers, against the rulers of the darkness of this world, against spiritual wickedness in high places. Wherefore take unto you the **whole armor of God, that ye might be able to withstand in the evil day and having done all to stand**. Ephesians 6:10-13.*

Many nuggets are found in this exhortation. **The devil has wiles; the many, different cunning craftiness he uses;** some of which we have examined already. We are to be fully armored; leaving nothing exposed. This is being meticulous in what we are doing, saying, and behaving: nothing is to be left uncovered. We are soldiers! We are exhorted **to stand twice; and to withstand once! We are not told to fight, but** we are to occupy or build up a garrison against the devil; for he has already been defeated! We are standing strong in the Lord; and **our stand is in the power of the might of God; and we do so in the evil day**. That is any time, we come under attack and when we are besieged.

In order to work out your own salvation; it is expedient that you know exactly what the whole armor of God is! Most preachers exhort believers to put on the armor of God; yet in 30 years as a believer I have heard fewer than two preachers who have actually clearly told us what the armor is. By the grace of God, this was one area where I had to diligently seek the Lord and search the Scripture to see the wisdom of God concerning this armor!

The devil tempted Jesus after forty days of fasting and prayer and when He hungered! Clothed in the whole armor of God, Jesus then modeled for us how to handle any temptation. He declared:

IT IS WRITTEN, MAN SHALL NOT LIVE BY BREAD ALONE, BUT BY EVERY WORD THAT PROCEEDETH OUT OF THE MOUTH OF GOD. (Matt. 4:4; Luke 4:4).

Jesus is always the Pattern! His answer to the devil's fierce tempting has had the answer in plain sight. Now an armor provides protection for a person from head to toe; so that bullets or other weaponry cannot infiltrate. Both "*it is written*" and "*every word that proceedeth out of the mouth of God*" is the **ARMOR** of God! Jesus was obviously fully clothed in the armor of God, and that was His answer every time the devil tempted Him. **The ARMOR is the WORD of GOD!** It behooves us to seriously take a look at this armor from head to toe! This includes shield, sword, lance, helmet, greaves and breastplate. This is crucial to your life's flow!

According as His divine power hath given unto us all things that pertain unto life and godliness, through the knowledge of Him that hath called us to glory and virtue.

Ephesians 6:14-18

Stand therefore, having your loins girt about with truth. (Vs. 14a) – The loins speak of that from which we reproduce. Everything we reproduce from within us must always bring forth the truth of God's Word! Jesus said, "*Sanctify them through thy truth: thy word is truth.*" (John 17:17). It is through the Word of God that you reproduce the things of God for your life and well-being.

and having on the breastplate of righteousness (Verse 14b). This covers our heart and soft organs. One's integrity, virtue, morality, purity of the things concerning one's life. Romans 1:17; 10:17 says:

For therein is the righteousness of God revealed from faith to faith: as it is written, the just shall live by faith. "

So then faith cometh by hearing, and hearing by the word of God.

 The righteousness of our Father comes to us through faith in the Word of Yahweh. The Word of God is that breastplate of right standing, right thinking and right actions. This mindset protects the issues of our soul/heart (morals, integrity, virtue).

And your feet shod with the preparation of the gospel of peace. (Verse 15)– Our feet are how we walk; we are to walk by the Word! The psalmist David declared: *Thy word is a lamp unto my feet, and a light unto my path* (Psalms 119:105). The gospel is the Word of God: the good news of our Almighty God and Father! The Word declares we have Peace with God and the peace of God so we no longer need to fear the enemy or our circumstances. Paul tells us that the gospel is the *"power of God unto salvation.* (Romans 1:16).

Above all, taking the shield of faith, wherewith ye shall be able to quench all the fiery darts of the wicked. (Verse 16)

This Scripture tells us that in our walk we will have fiery darts thrown at us from the wicked- around us! We are to have a force shield around us at all times! This "shield" is made of faith: the faith of God; faith in God; and your faith! Faith comes through the Word of God! Faith is that supernatural Kingdom substance through which we access the promises of God for us. Roms.10:17 states:

Now faith cometh by hearing, and hearing by the word of God

The Apostle Peter tells us that we are given, *"exceeding great and precious promises: that by these ye might be partakers of the divine nature.* (2 Peter 1:4). In order to partake of Christ's divine nature, we ought to have the word/promises of God front and center in our mouths. For we access these promises by faith: and that is our protective shield! Faith assures us that in Christ, we are already set:

Far above all principality, and power, and might, and dominion, and every name that is named. (Ephesians 1:21) Hallelujah!

And take the helmet of salvation, and the sword of the Spirit,

which is the word of God: Praying always with all prayer and supplication in the Spirit, and watching thereunto with all perseverance and supplication for all saints. (Verses 17- 18)

The helmet covers our head and neck! This covers our mind, which is housed in the soul, the seat of our thoughts, our emotions, beliefs and our will; the whole personality! It also covers our eyes, ears, nose and mouth, thus covering how we see, hear, intuit and speak! The Word of God sets the paradigm of the Kingdom of Heaven; and ought to form all our perceptions, thoughts, ideas, and concepts. It brings transformation to the soul, bringing it into subjection to Spirit. As we live, move and breath the Word of God, it supplies the power of God to walk out our salvation (Roms.1:16).

Instead of knowing that the whole armor is indeed the Word of God; we have limited only the sword of the Spirit to be so. The Word of God is the full weaponry of God against the enemy! As the two-edged sword the Word both cuts the works of the enemy, as well as a tool of healing for us

The believer's arsenal includes various different types of prayer for different times.Regardless of the kind of prayer one uses; [whether intercession, the prayer of thanksgiving, of binding and loosing, the prayer of agreement, petition, or the prayer of faith]: these prayers are to be **Holy Spirit led! We are to pray the Word of God back to the Father, both in tongues, and in articulate language.**

Supplication is the asking; the posture of the heart in prayer. There is humility and intensity in praying that way, with the awareness that the Kingdom of Heaven delivers answers! It is militant yet humble. Jesus addressed the believer's power to bind the strongman and spoil his goods (Mark 3:27); now that we have been both raised up as well as made to sit with Christ in the heavenlies. (Ephesians 2:5,6)! That "sit" is prophetic of the finished work of Christ. There is no agitation, no nervousness and no fear! Just as our Father rested from His works (Gens.2:2); Jesus sat down! Amen! We become the very rest of our Father, as we too experientially rest in Jesus far above principalities, powers and every name!

There are three areas in which you and I will be tempted and buffeted as the Apostle John showed us in 1John 2:16:

For all that is in the world, the lust of the flesh, and the lust of the eyes, and the pride of life, is not of the Father, but is of the world.

Eve was tempted in these three, and Jesus Himself, being man; was tempted likewise. Well, so are we: you and I, every day! It is only the Word of our God that protects us every time! As the Body of Christ we often like saying, **every tongue that shall rise against us is condemned:** as if God is the One doing the condemning. Not so! It is you and I who does the condemning (Isaiah 54:17). This is our heritage; and this is right in the sight of our Father Creator!

*No weapon that is formed against thee shall prosper, and every tongue that shall rise against thee in judgement **thou** shalt condemn. This is the heritage of the servants of the Lord and their righteousness is of me saith the Lord. Amen! Selah!*

Jesus told us in Mark 11:22-24 to believe what we say because we are to be saying only the things of God! This is having the faith of God, which must precede what we say. Remember the creation story when darkness and void was everywhere. The Creator spoke; and He created what He needed. That is what Jesus modeled for us when tempted by the devil. He answered the onslaughts of satan with *It is written*. Only **when you speak the Word of God are you fully armored!** We dismantle our own belief in God's Word by speaking wrong things and agreeing with the kingdom of darkness.

The only things we should believe are the things we say with our mouths, because like Jesus, we should always answer with the Word! Have you been using perverse words? Did you think that perverse only meant cussing, immorality or sexually deviant? Perhaps you judged yourself more righteous than the world? Truth is, from a biblical Kingdom perspective, we have been a perverse generation; by our unbelief, evidenced by our faithless words. Those have corroded and rendered God's Word inoperative in our lives.

Consider this: in the discourse recorded in Matthew16:1-4 this group of religious leaders asked Jesus for a sign. Jesus addressed that by **calling them a perverse generation**. Now how in the world is that perverse? What could be wrong with asking for a sign? Yet if we look at what perversity means, we clearly see from Jesus' perspective where they were coming from. These people, just like the Church of today, doubted God's words, always wanting a sign, much as we constantly seek confirmation for everything. One time a man brought his lunatic son to Jesus's disciples, but they could not cast out the devils. The father then cried out desperately to Jesus for help. Jesus answered the man saying and addressing the situation:

O faithless and perverse generation... (Matthew 17:17-21).

What? PERVERSE? Jesus called them perverse because they doubted God's Word as well as their own power as sons of Yahweh, who had been given dominion on Earth! The disciples later asked Jesus and was told that their **unbelief** stopped them from casting out the devil, and *this kind goeth not out but by prayer and fasting.*

The prayer and fasting here has more to do with **getting rid of our unbelief in God's Word; than in "getting power" to cast out devils** as is mostly preached by the Church! That is only one measure! Hear the full oracles of God! In Jesus**, you are a king, born with authority whether you fast or not! Fasting rids us of amnesia of who we were created to be; and of the filth of our unbelief!** Prayer and fasting energizes the power within us, opens up our eyes, and realigns us to our Kingdom mandate to be deliverers of mankind! Fasting energizes us, not our Father! Fasting does shows our Heavenly Father our total dependence upon His power, and His Kingdom! Matt.6:13 says

For thine is the kingdom, and the power, and the Glory, forever....

The conclusion of the matter is this: putting on the full armor of God is aligning our mouths with the Word of God! Father *upholds all things by the Word of His power* (Heb.1:3); *esteems His word above His name (Ps.138:2) and watches over His word to perform it* (Jer.1:12)! We ought to only speak the Word in all things: of Who Yahweh is; what He has said; and who we are in Him! The result is multiplied growth and abounding more and more in the knowledge of God! Creation is waiting; our Father is waiting!

Let the words of my mouth, and the meditation of my heart, be acceptable in thy sight, O LORD, my strength and my redeemer

PART IV

STUPID PRAYERS
& NAÏVE SAYINGS

CHAPTER 18

STUPID PRAYERS

How many times have you heard a saint say, "You have got to pray through?" I remember hearing that as a young neophyte and wondering what that meant. I had been listening to Kenneth and Gloria Copeland teachings on faith, and was being birth from that realm, so it perturbed me. Yet that statement was and still is so pervasive in the Body! On television and radio, I still repeatedly hear, "you need to pray through" or "you need to get a prayer through." Those statements are almost always followed by the famous scripture stating how the prince of Persia tried to block Daniel's prayer until Michael the Archangel intervened.

Had I not been hearing faith from the Copelands, I would no doubt have thought that it was very difficult to get answers to my prayers. Are those statements just religious things we say in church? Are they perverse? They sound good, but do they present the full counsel of God? We must understand that good can be the enemy of best and that is a thirty- fold measure! (Chapter1). Regardless of what you've heard from your favorite preacher, let's examine that "sacred cow" in light of Biblical doctrine

but without faith it is impossible to please Him: for he that cometh to God must believe that He is, and that He is a rewarder of them that diligently seek Him. (Hebrews 11:6)

When Moses asked God about His name; Yahweh answered:

I AM THAT I AM: and He said, Thus shalt thou say unto the children of Israel, I AM hath sent me unto you (Exo.3:14)

Whenever you need anything and approach God in prayer, your first priority must be that you **know** for certain that I AM is there;

that I AM hears you; and that I AM will reward you as you seek Him diligently. Yahweh is I AM; He is always in the now, always present; always available and ready; and as Father, His delight is to answer our prayers. Therefore, we can:

come boldly to the throne of grace, that we might obtain mercy, and find grace to help in time of need." (Heb.4:16).

Clearly then, once your belief system is sure that God is there and available, there is a peaceful rest as you realize that God does indeed hear you; and will grant your petitions. That is faith! It is that intangible substance; a title deed of your request. When you say that you need to "get a prayer through**" there is that predisposition to believe that your prayers are being blocked**; that perhaps God will not hear you; and most certainly, a belief that perhaps God won't grant your petition. That is both soulish and unscriptural; and is thus a leaven of the Pharisees (see Chap.6).

Hebrews 11:6 *without faith it is impossible to please God* never looks at the negative. It sounds like war consciousness to expect that when you pray there will always be some major opposition. That expectation is in contrast to what Jesus told us. He also declared:

if ye abide in me and my Word abide in thee, thou shall ask what ye will and ye will receive (John 15:7).

if two of you shall agree on earth, as touching anything that they shall ask, it shall be done for them of my Father which is in heaven" (Matt 18:19).

There is no mention at all that we would have to "pray through." Matter of fact, we are promised answered prayers, so that our joy might be full. Father God delights in answering our prayers! God is Light; all that pertains to Him is clothed in light and illumination. **Jesus at no time, ever even alluded to, that perhaps there is a need to "pray through" or to persevere in your own strength. In** Hebrews 11:6 says rather that: ***he that cometh to God must know that He is..*** That means that it really doesn't matter who tries to block your prayers: but that God is there! The LORD, our Father; He is I AM—present, able, ready—and the only qualification to reach Him is faith; Simply recognizing that God is there; that He **is I AM,** is faith. Amen.

It means that we don't need to get through walls, ceilings or principalities—not when we are in the Kingdom of Heaven ; for we are seated with Christ at God's right hand!

far above principality and power and might and dominion and every name that is named. (Ephesians 1:21), Selah!

if we know that He hear us, whatsoever we ask, we know that we have the petitions that we desired of Him. 1 John5:15.

And it shall come to pass that before they call, I will answer, and while they are yet speaking, I will hear as Isaiah 65:24 says!

How utterly beautiful! Before you call—Daddy answers! Daddy delights to answer our prayers! That is one great promise concerning the coming millennial kingdom; **which you get to access through your assertive declaration of "thy kingdom come, thy will be done on earth as it is in heaven." Wow!** You should order your conversation based on the Word of God, without any doubt, for you will have what you say!

In Hebrews 12:1, after a lengthy exhortation about saints who exercised tremendous faith: we are admonished to "*lay aside every weight and the sin that so easily besets us; looking unto Jesus the author and finisher of our faith."*

Awesome! What then, is the sin that so easily beset us? **It is the lack of faith!** That is it, plain and simple! A lack of faith is what we ought to constantly war against—not satan! We then constantly engage an old enemy: and look to him in blame, when our Lord has already defeated him and stripped him of all the power [he had] in heaven and earth! Scripture also says that we should "*fight the good fight of faith; lay hold of eternal life." (1Tim 6:12).* Since you have Holy Spirit Who is the **spirit of faith,** the words coming out of your mouth will tell us about your own belief system! For *we also believe, and therefore speak (*2 Cor. 4:13).

We cannot say we believe God and then say things that are contrary to Scripture. Disagreement with God is agreement with the kingdom of darkness. There is no gray area! It is the kingdom of darkness versus the Kingdom of God. The Word of God settles it.

"Lord I believe, help thou my unbelief." Mark 9:23

That precious man presented himself with honesty and so much vulnerability! I love this man! Maybe a particular issue is no longer present in one area of your life because you have come to a place of victory and maturity in that area. Yet in another area, you may have a real struggle in the daily application and fleshing out of the truth of the Word of God. **That unbelief is the struggle of the carnal mind against the mind of Christ!** You might even feel a struggle when considering some of the things in this book, so I invite you to search out the Scriptures, that you might:

work out your own salvation with fear and trembling." Phil 2:12.

This weight- this "besetting sin" that easily wears you down, causes you to struggle and be double minded, rendering you unable to receive anything from God. For this reason, we are exhorted:

Be ye transformed by the renewing of your mind, that ye may prove what is that good and acceptable and perfect will of God. Roms12:2

It is only a transformed mind that can test/approve the will of God; a carnal mind is good for nothing but to be dung for the fodder (Roms8:6). The Word of God must be applied at all cost! Your life will have fewer struggles, as you become more intentional in what you say, for indeed you will most certainly have what you say. (Mark 11:24). We are told to mix the word with faith and have:

heaven upon the earth" (Deut.11:21)

If you truly believe that your prayers reach only as far as the ceiling; why is that? God is Omnipresent, Omnipotent and totally Omniscient! So, do your prayers have to go farther than the ceiling? Or do your prayers have to be faith-filled prayers? Is it where your prayers go; or rather Who you believe on and what you are saying?

And this is the confidence that we have in Him, that if we ask anything according to His will, He heareth us (1John 5:14).

What is this utter nonsense about ceilings and praying through then? That is a stupid prayer! The great qualifier is this: What we are asking for must be based on the will/Word of God. He has *esteemed His word over His Name* (Ps.138:2) and He *watches over His Word to perform it* (Jer. 1:12). Can I just say; "Oh my goodness?!" That's grounds for shouting right there! Hallelujah! Get a prayer through?

Seriously! I know it is a Churchy sacred cow; but that deviates from the nature of Jehovah; and is thus truly perverse! It misrepresents Father's heart! Why don't you judge for yourself!

We need to repent from the senseless striving we have been doing in Church; for Jesus said, *"My yoke is easy, and my burden is light"* (Matthew 11:30). It is time to stop the constant struggle we give ourselves by engaging a weakened, defeated foe! We must put away the froward mouth and perverse [lips] words from us.

Making the Word of God of none effect through your tradition, which you have delivered: and many such like things you do. (Mk.7:13).

Let us bring a balance here! We are citizens of the Kingdom of Heaven. Amen! Through the blood of Jesus and the power of the resurrection, the Kingdom of Heaven is available to us; now! We are surrounded by the wicked kingdom of darkness, which always presses up against the Kingdom of Heaven. Both kingdoms are spiritual kingdoms, and because we live in this physical earth realm; there is a stress; a buffeting that we feel; and more so as evil and darkness increases. As we stand on earth to pray; there is always that tangible foreboding feeling all around, that might cause you to doubt what the Word says. Our heavenly Daddy Who is Divine Omniscience; knew this! He told us to declare *"thy kingdom come, thy will be done on earth as it is in heaven.* This is our covering! In the Kingdom of Heaven, there is no stress and buffeting. Isaiah 9:7 says:

Of the increase of his government and peace there shall be no end

I AM JUST A WORM OF THE EARTH/THE HEART IS DECEITFUL?

I have heard too many preachers go on about being a filthy worm of the earth; and that the heart is deceitful and desperately wicked. **That has got to be some of the most perverse prayers/sayings I have heard over the last thirty years.** It is full of ego and just plain stupid. Bear in mind that stupid means: "foolish, ignorant, unintelligent, and dense" to name a few. Seriously, I get it that up until Jesus; in Adam, we had all fall short of the glory; and we were all wicked evil sinners. Yet throughout all Scripture, our Father never left His children!

His redemptive plan was always seen in types and shadows under the Old Covenant. **The first Passover showed us God's plan for man's redemption; in an unblemished lamb, sacrificed for the** freedom of all who would put their faith in Him. Just as Israel was spared from death by applying the blood of the lamb over the door, Jesus the true Lamb paid the price at the cross by shedding His blood for our sins. John the Baptist recognized Him and declared in *John 1:29:*

Behold the Lamb of God who takes away the sin of the world.

The Son of God became the son of man, so the sons of men could become sons of God! Question is: did Jesus die so we could be worms of the earth? I did, and still believe the truth that we were created higher than worms! Yes, we were all of us in a lousy and depraved place: the condition of a worm and totally polluted in our own blood (Job 25:4; Ps.22:6; Isa 41:14). Yet, it was while we were in condition of a worm (unclean, unrighteous,filthy), that Christ loved us, washed us in His blood and died for us (Roms.5:8). Amen!

Thanks be to our God and Father; for this grace teaches our hearts to reverence Him. This Jesus the Christ, was resurrected for our glory! Father *raised him from the dead; and set Him at His own right hand in the heavenly places; far above all principalities, and every name. (Eph.1:20, 21)!* **That He did suffer and died for us, to be worms; and with deceitful and wicked hearts? How utterly perverse!** Was this all in vain? Is this the mind of Christ we have been given? On no occasion at all did Jesus declare Himself to be a worm! God the Father however did openly declare Him, Praise God!

Concerning his Son Jesus Christ our Lord, which was made of the seed of David according to the flesh; and declared to be the Son of God with power, according to the spirit of holiness, by the resurrection from the dead (Romans1:3-4)

The resurrection was a result of the power of God Almighty; and the resurrection ushered in Holy Spirit! Post Calvary, we are now neither down trodden nor filthy. In Jesus Christ, the Resurrection: we too have been made to "stand up." We do also get to sit with

Jesus in heavenly places! Yeah!

For the Father *"hath raised us up together and made us sit together in heavenly places in Christ Jesus." (Eph.2:6).*

Coupled with obliteration of our sin nature, God promised us a new heart (Eze.11:19, 20; 36:26). This was available through His Son Jesus, the moment He was resurrected. This new heart one receives at confessing one's faith in Jesus! I was given a new heart! It is now: *"Christ in you, the hope of glory (Col.1:27).* Glory! Yes glory! In the fall,mankind sinned and fell short of God's glory (Roms.3:23). Now as citizens of the Kingdom of Heaven, we have been reconciled to God; and now we are ambassadors (2Cor.5:20) representing our King and country. Glory is now our portion!

As such: you have credentials with heaven's honor (Isa.43:4). Ambassadors speak for and on behalf of the country they represent! The Kingdom of Heaven is endured with power, glory and might, and its representatives also carry authority which reflect its nature! How utterly stupid and perverse to assume to think that as a "worm" you might dare to re-present our Almighty God, Creator, and King?

Any teaching, preaching/utterance which say we have deceitful, wicked hearts; or claim we are worms; post Calvary, is perverse, evil and stupid! This is an example of *"evil communications [which] corrupt good manners" (1Cor.15:33).* **Rather than live as kings of the earth; far too many believers have heard and believed this evil!** Filled with false humility, they have languished below purpose; leading mediocre, beggarly lives; and have totally misrepresented our Glorious King, Father and God!

Enough with all that which contradicts the finished work of the Cross, and spits in the face of the accomplishment of the resurrected Christ, and is just plain trash talk! My heart is not deceitful and desperately wicked; and I am certainly not a worm of the earth! I am not agreeing with that at any cost. Enough said! As I work out my salvation with fear and trembling, I totally agree with and say what Scripture says about me: **I am the righteousness of God in Christ Jesus** (2Cor.5:21)! satan certainly see us as the righteousness of God in Christ. The question is: do you see yourself thus?

Lord, we believe; help Thou our unbelief.

CHAPTER 19

NAÏVE SAYINGS

SINNER OR SAINT?

One of the most popular sayings of the last few years has been "We fall down, and we get up; and a saint is just a sinner, who fell down, and got up!" One has to consider the nature of God in everything and at all times. I was a sinner before I was born again: because I had the nature to sin. When I was born again I received a new nature; a new heart; and now sin no longer have dominion over me. Romans 6:14. Amen!

At redemption, there was an exchange, and my sin nature was nailed to the cross. Jesus died in two ways—for me and as me! I received righteousness as my new nature and I consequently became the *righteousness of God;* (2Corinthians 5:21). Even though I do occasionally sin, I no longer have that old sin nature (1John 3:5, 6). I am called a saint, because I have a righteousness nature and I have a righteousness consciousness. Yahweh our God and Father is most certainly not schizophrenic, and neither ought we to be! We are all born again in image and likeness of God. There is no duality at all!

When we say that a saint is a sinner, we deny the work of the Cross, and the blood of Jesus Christ that obliterated the sin nature of mankind. We are virtually saying that we now have two natures. Sounds like when we fall we are sinners, and when we get back up we are saints? I don't know! Judge for yourself!

What I do know is what Scripture says and what its principles point to. This is clear: Father and Son do not work against each other. Jesus says, *"I and My Father are one"* (John 10:30). The Father did not send His Son to die so we could keep that old sinful heart. So categorically, we who are born again are no longer sinners, because we no longer possess that old sinner nature. Of course, we miss the mark; as we are in process of renewing the whole mind! Believers in the plight of the very constant resistance coming from the kingdom of darkness; miss the mark from time to time.

The truth is there are two kingdoms in conflict—the Kingdom of GOD and the kingdom of darkness. Both are spiritual kingdoms. The kingdom of darkness is ruled by a Darth Vader-like character called satan; whose desire is to be like the Most High God! satan's kingdom constantly jockeys for ruler-ship over the Kingdom of Heaven. Blood-washed believers living in an evil age; constantly feel the turmoil; and at times miss the mark in our responses. In its simplicity sin means "missing the mark." Our soul struggles to align with our spirit; and we sin; that doesn't mean that we still have that old sin nature. What it means is that the mind needs renewing in that area! **What we struggle with, is the negatives which are yet a part of one's carnal mind; and upon which the enemy feeds**. As you grow in grace, through the Word of God; and go from faith to faith and strength to strength, you experientially show that sin no longer has dominion over you.

DELIVER US FROM EVIL

Evil is one favorite subject in the Church, it implies negativity and darkness and one immediately think of the devil! satan is the father of all things evil, no doubt; although Jesus never said **deliver us from satan. He did say** *"deliver us from evil"* **(Matthew 6:13) though! Dictionary meaning of e**vil means wicked, unfortunate, harmful. Let us look at evil from a different paradigm. When Jesus's disciples asked Him for a lesson on prayer, He proceeded to teach them, detail upon detail: the Kingdom paradigm of prayer.

Jesus told us to "say" in our prayer: addressing our Father as Abba/ Daddy: for this is Who the Lord is! Already we realize that we are now in our heavenly Daddy's protected care. Our Father is the Lord of the whole Earth; thus, we ascribe worth, and worship, and honor and strength and power to Him. Next in line; we are to usher in [by speaking] God's kingdom to the Earth; and for God's will to be done. His kingdom comes by declaration!

As believers, one must and will relate to other believers, the ungodly, sinners and heathens! With this comes violations, hurt, misunderstandings; levels of pain; and trauma, and so you will need to constantly forgive others. As kings we ask for forgiveness, and we forgive others as well. For we all offend by omission as well as by commission. The daily walk of the believer will involve hills and valleys; desert times, with many detours, some stop signs and dead ends, as well as times of smooth sailing! With all these we are prone to temptation; thus we ask our Father who is all Seeing and all Knowing, to help us to avoid the many traps and pits along the way.

We are to also ask our Father God, for deliverance from evil. Biblically: evil means labors, bad, annoyances, hardships, wicked, hurtful, vile, useless; and any deviation from God's holy nature. We do know that evil is satan's domain! Jesus desires for us to understand the different wiles of the enemy, so he on purpose did not say "deliver us from satan." Post Calvary, **evil manifests in our lives from things we think, speak, believe or do.** Now based on many things frequently heard and seen within the Body of Christ, it does appear that believers often speak more about satan than they do about Jesus! It seems like believers are really, very troubled about the operations of the enemy in their daily lives more than they are in the victory of the resurrected Christ. From a biblical, kingdom standpoint, that of itself, is evil!

On another level; and when we look at evil as uselessness, as vile or wicked, we begin to see how our communication is too often evil! For that which questions God's heart and integrity is PERVERTED; and is thus useless, vile and evil. **When we walk or speak in speech or conduct which refuses to see the good of Yahweh's heart, or His promises, that is evil. Doubting his power, authority, dominion, and the responsibility we have been given through Jesus; those things are considered evil in God's eyes!** Disciples are necessarily held accountable in this prayer: to maintain dependence upon our King Supreme: Who is our Heavenly Father!

Father; deliver us from the evil of contradicting your Name, your Nature; and your Word: for Thine is the kingdom, Amen!

HE DON'T ALWAYS COME WHEN WE WANT HIM BUT HE'S ALWAYS ON TIME!

That is another of those stupid prevailing lies that we frequently o hear being preached; while scores of ignorant believers languish under the false belief that there are moments when Father God will on purpose just cause us to sweat in abandonment and rejection. That is an evil thought and needs be repented of! Fact is, people tend to not trust another when they feel that they are being judged or when they are not being heard. The mindset is that God is often unavailable to His children; and comes only right in the nick of time after we have been toiling and sweating. Not only is that traumatizing to think about...it is a wicked perverted lie!

It very much belies the nature and character of God our Father and satisfies our own un-forgiveness, and often mistrust towards Him. Deuteronomy 31:6 declares *"and the Lord, He it is that doth go before thee; He will be with thee, He will not fail thee, neither forsake thee: fear not, neither be dismayed."*

We are also told in His Word, that *before we call He answers (Isa.65:24).* Additionally, Jesus stated in His prayer to the Father regarding another Comforter, that Holy Spirit would *abide with you forever.* This is a guarantee that we would never be comfortless (John 14:16). How very nerve racking to even think otherwise! Not only ought we therefore to repent for believing the lie that we are neglected until right "in the nick of time." Faith knows that we are heard, and because we are heard we have *confidence that our petition is granted according to His will (1John5:14-15).* Our Father is Omnipresent, and the Kingdom of God is within us! In the economy of the Kingdom of Heaven, there is no time! Time started in Genesis 1:5; when the evening and the morning was the first day. Time is measured only on Earth: *"a time to every purpose under the heaven" (Eccls3:1)*

We set time and such limits on our Father the Creator of time! Time is the Father's idea, and time is in God! The Kingdom of God is a relationship between our Loving Heavenly Daddy and us His children! Our Daddy delights in us! Any other declaration is perverse! He rejoices over us with singing; He is always there! Always! Thanks be to the Father: our Daddy God!

CHAPTER 20

NAIVETY

CAN WE HAVE A CONVERSATION?

Have you ever casually asked a believer a simple question: perhaps about his/her plans or desires, and you received an answer which sounded something like this: **"I'm just waiting on the Lord"** or **"the Lord's will be done,"** or **"whatever the Lord wants me to do?"** I've heard those responses and I'm sure you have as well. Maybe you have even said something like that yourself. I am pretty sure I did myself say that in my immature years.

There is this sense of rejection from those "super religious answers" from well-meaning believers who love Jesus as much as they know how. What I know for sure is that an answer like that almost always kills any conversation. What else can one say after having heard, "Whatever God wants for me?"

I have found myself repeatedly marveling at how unapproachable believers can be at times. I have found that believers tend to not have really good, normal conversations; where you can share your desire and plans with one another; in a manner of friendship and camaraderie. Leaving everything up to God sounds sweet; and humble; but it is unbiblical! It takes away our responsibility for stewarding the Earth and from being fruitful and multiplying in every direction. In the Church world, it seems the mindset is that a person is not supposed to have any kind of desire or passion. Many seem to feel that since God gives us everything, we are not supposed to dream, to aspire to do anything, especially in the world, unless God literally tells us to do it.

That just doesn't add up! It can't make spiritual sense that God gave us free will, gave us His principles, precepts and statutes to govern our lives, yet He tells us every single thing we ought to do. Even though God gave us dominion, many believe they shouldn't even choose a vocation because God will always choose for us. Certainly, He guides us, making us aware of our God-given gifts, talents and calling; but we also can choose. There are numerous times when Daddy will specifically tell us exactly what we are to do for sure! The point is that we are co-laborers together with our Father and what we want matters to Him, because He is Father; and Father cares! Our son-ship lies in our ability to be led by our Father; and in having Father's heart.

As a result of skewed thinking, there is often no real conversation between believers concerning things which might be stirring in our hearts. We have often missed one fundamental aspect of why we are called the Church; and thus we've become voiceless, and I believe very unbiblical. Church is for conversation and connection. Without conversation, there can be no real fellowship. Everything happens around conversation, and every single thing that we do in our lives on earth, starts with a conversation. Everything! **Man was created around, as well as for conversation;** and that is clearly seen in the beginning when God Creator spoke with the Godhead in *"let us make man."* You and I were born from a conversation; between two people; whether negative or positive; it took some level of conversation; spoken or unspoken.

CAN WE HAVE DESIRES ON OUR OWN?

delight thyself also in the Lord and He shall give thee the desires of thine heart. Commit thy way unto the Lord, trust also in Him; and He shall bring it to pass. (Psalm 37:4-5)

Desire is a strong wishing, a strong wanting for something. Clearly then, the Father expects us to have desires. Because the Church has cut itself off from having any desires or dreams of its own, we have missed the beautiful heart of our heavenly Father. As recorded in Genesis 11, when the people began to converse around what they desired to do; it became so big that God had to come down and stop it; for their desire was the product of the soul and was thus ungodly! Remember, that once the soul begins to rule, then beezebub multiplies that thinking; for it is product of the carnal mind. We have thwarted that Scripture to mean that any desire a believer has will be evil. Thus, the adversary has used that to skew his orphan spirit into the carnal mind of multiplied believers; resulting in a lack of our ability to converse around a common goal.

The word *de-sire* itself translates in the **wish of the Father- the King.** *De-* means of: and *sire* means- the father/king. We should arise and know that the many amazing desires you and I have felt were birthed in our spirits by the Father Himself. Amen! You are *joined to the Lord[and]is one spirit"* (1Cor.6:17); so the very things which stirs Daddy's heart; stirs your heart as well. **For the essence of son-ship, is that sons are led by the Spirit of God!** Son-ship is being, not doing! Son-ship is a quality of spirit; and is not gender based. Women are sons as well; for in Christ there is neither male or female (Gal.3:8); and men make up, and are a part of the Bride of Christ.

As the breathing living Body of Christ, we are a network of conversation. Jesus Himself was a conversationalist. He chatted, fellowshipped, and inter-reacted with all kinds of people. You are developed through conversation, and when you are not able to talk about the things in your hearts; and when you walk alone; then you have walled off your own creativity. Groups form around conversation, and the Church is a place of and for connection! We connect through conversation. As sons, **we are given different gifts to facilitate our diverse dreams, so we can evolve and grow, and so that we would need each other.** Conversation is optimal then.

One perverse way the enemy has comes in; is to keep believers so imprisoned that some actually believe that if you tell your brother about your dreams; then he/she will work against you to keep you from accomplishing that dream or desire. So we reject each other; and clamor in fear and suspicion against the brethren, not rightly discerning the mystical Body of Christ: which we all are a part of. This is perverse within the Body of Christ and fosters the "spirit of Cain" to be released and perpetuated within our midst. This is never the heart of God for his sons! Fellowship involves conversation; fellowship involves connection. 1John1:7 states:

But if we walk in the light [transparency, illumination], *as He is in the light, we have fellowship one with another, and the Blood of Jesus Christ His son cleanse us from all unrighteousness.*

When you share your dreams and desires, your brother can hold a space for you; in prayer and encouragement. When you live from that space where you depend on and need each other; it teaches you to become your brother's keeper! Together both can become more effective in the world at large; as each become a space for possibility for the other! You become I -AM- Possible; for with God nothing shall be impossible. On the other hand, when there is mistrust and fear, the enemy is at work. Working out your own salvation also involves relating to your brothers; as you mirror back to your brother his behaviors and attitudes; as he does to you.

Counsel in the heart of a man is like deep waters, but a man of understanding will draw it out.

You can stunt your own growth; for your growth is tested around your brethren. You flesh out your "transformation" as you give and receive feedback. When you share, talk about, and pray with your brethren about your dreams and desires; and his aspirations; you both actually get to judge the secrets of your own hearts and your brother's heart. Cain was jealous of his brother and killed him. Unlike Cain, both you and the sister, might be able to honestly recognize negative, outlaw feelings of jealousy, covetousness and envy; which flow from the carnal mind; as they surface!

Do nothing out of rivalry or conceit, but in humility consider others better as more important than yourselves. Phillipians2:3

You get to renew your mind when you practice through the Word of God, to be pure and honest towards each other. You both get to *"confess your faults one to another, and pray one for another that ye may be healed"* (James 5:16)! Transformation will fill both your souls; Amen! God has already placed all your potential on the inside of you; He gives you gifts as it pleases Him; so there is no room for jealousy! You and your brother are both valuable in each other's transformation and destiny. You cannot know yourself by yourself; but through the eyes of others. This too is covenantal!

Jesus went off by Himself to spend time with His Father, as a habit. You ought to do likewise! The other times, He was always surrounded by His companions, and other people. He had the masses, the seventy he sent out to minister; and he had the twelve disciples he walked with. Then there was the three; Peter, James and John; He took them places He didn't take the other nine (Mk.5:37; 9:2). Then there was the one: John the beloved; who leaned upon Jesus breast, hearing his very heart beat. All those are patterns of relationships, which you need to carve out in your own life, with the brethren.

When you stay by yourself; and walk alone, you tend to walk more in darkness. When and if stagnant emotions of the carnal mind come up; they can multiply within your soul, lurk upon you, and cause you to manifest ungodly behaviors. Walking alone, keeps you from being accountable to others, and fosters an orphan spirit.

God places the solitary in families: He bringeth out those which are bound with chains but the rebellious dwell in a dry land. Psa. 68:6

Believers need much more balance as it relates to the many desires of our hearts. The revelation that we are so in union with the Father, that the things we do and say pleases Daddy's heart is bread for the soul. So, is there a place where God ends and where you begin? We are sons, so *in all thy [our ways] we acknowledge God (Pro 3:5-6)! Thus* we no longer have to be afraid to have desires, or to talk about them; for our choices are empowered by Holy Spirit; thus making Daddy's heart real glad.

As mentioned before Jehovah did not correct Adam as he named the animals! He offered no input: He just watched Adam lovingly! Yet, we who are sons of God have gotten to the place where we can not even make a life decision! That suspicion that the Father "may not come when you want Him" fosters fear and mistrust within your soul! When you have not clothed yourself enough in the mind of Christ; you often become forgetful of your inheritance in Christ! Jesus said: *Father hath not left me alone; for I do always those things that please Him."*

WHAT OF EDUCATION

In the meantime, the Church too often has refused to educate itself; but have looked to escape this wicked world in the ultimate rapture of the Church! We have shown no real passion and panting desire to transform a world except to sell "fire insurance" so folks will escape hell's fire. As a result; much ground was taken by the enemy when the Church stood at the "hallelujah bus stop" expecting to be taken out of here. Thus, the Church did not set trained and worthy people in high offices of influence! **We are told that the prince of Persia intercepted Daniel's prayer, and this became an anthem within the Church world to expect trouble every time we pray.** What was not usually explained is that Daniel was a highly-placed, educated man in Babylon; and that he did interpret the king's dream, and affected a whole nation!

We know the story of Shadrach, Meshach and Abednego: young men who did not bow to the gods of Babylon. Yet we have failed to speak into the hearts of our young people that they too can go far and deep into kings' houses in service; and be taught in the wisdom of Egypt even while God sustains them. Moses was educated in Pharaoh's house and Joseph was taught in the things of Egypt.

These are powerful precepts! David also went from herding the sheep to playing the harp for king Saul! He was getting practice on how to care for and rule over God's people. The Church has been rather naïve; in failing to consider enough, that one must be taught in the skills of; and understand the systems of the world in preparation for being placed in positions of influence and authority; to affect change on a wider level. *(Matt 10:16) says:*

be ye therefore wise as serpents, and harmless as doves

Mostly, we have not been **encouraged to have big lofty dreams, and so we have not been able to take mountains as a restorative act as sons of Yahweh** (Luke 4:5,6). Thus, we have lagged behind the work of effectively transforming the world. Nonetheless; it is now covertly happening; for our *God will finish the work and cut it short in righteousness (Rom9:28).* We do play a part: yet we have been waiting for God to tell us what to dream. In the meantime, we have ignored the truth that our Father patiently waits to hear the dreams, which beat upon the hearts of his sons in the earth. *For* we are *"laborers together with God"* (1 Cor.3:9) Amen!

CHAPTER 21

THE LORD'S WILL BE DONE
"GOD IS IN CONTROL!"

God's original plan has never changed; He still expects His man to have dominion, and to dress and manage the earth (Genesis 1:27; 2:15). It is important to understand that God on purpose locked Himself out of the Earth realm: and He sent His Son Jesus, as the Pattern for us. Jesus is the model for us on how to bring the Kingdom of Heaven into the midst of suffering, hungry humanity. Through Jesus Christ, Yahweh trusts His sons with His authority and dominion. Father God fully expects us to mature and be the deliverers of the Earth: doing good as did Jesus; (Acts 10:38) and shining the light for men to see Him.

Yahweh rules the heavens! However, He gave this earth to us, the sons of men to run. (Ps.115:16). At the fall of man, the earth was cursed, down to the ground. Since then, all of creation, both man and beast; have been waiting in travail; a stressful, painful kind of ordeal. Although mankind is mostly unaware; there is yet a deep longing for super-heroes to come forth, and bring deliverance and restore peace. The Holman translation reads:

For the creation eagerly wait with anticipation for God's sons to be revealed [manifestation] (Roms.8:19).

As the Church overcomes the evil of our disbelief in who Yahweh says we are; then we can get on with the business of managing the Earth and delivering men. Manifestation begins with "man." It is a demonstration of men with god-like qualities; men of power, men of authority; demi-gods! The sons of Yah are the super-heroes mankind waits for!

All of us love to watch block buster movies of deliverers and super-heroes who rise up and restore peace and tranquility! Whether it is X-men or Transformers; Superman; Guardians of the Galaxy or Black Panther; we all love when good triumph over evil. Great and small, we love super-heroes because deep inside each of us lies a deliverer. We get to live vicariously through them in the movies, and the other media outlet; while our hearts swell within us; with both joy and longing! For we also groan within ourselves; to stand tall and be counted among the brave, as the Lion of the tribe of Judah roars from within us!

Make no mistake, Jehovah God has supreme control; but He left man with delegated authority to both dress and keep the earth (Gen.2:15). He also waits: for His mature sons to arise in power and kingly authority, bringing deliverance to mankind, and demonstrate to this dying world just Who the God of Heaven truly is. God's intention has remained steadfast and unchangeable throughout the ages; and He waits in expectation:

To the intent that now unto the principalities and powers in heavenly places might be known by the Church the diverse [wisdom] intelligence of God. (Eph.3:10). Selah!

IS GOD'S WILL ALWAYS DONE ON EARTH?

Not really! That sounds like blasphemy, doesn't it? God's will is only always done in Heaven, the realm of His Eternal Kingdom! However, since Adam handed over his dominion to the evil usurper; the will of God is not always done on earth! When asked how we ought to pray: Jesus instructed His disciples to pray by saying:

thy kingdom come, thy will be done on earth as it is in heaven (Matt.6:10; Lk.11:2),

There would be no need to pray for God's will to be done on Earth if that was truth. Any prayer then, which doesn't invite the Kingdom to come in our midst is pretty incomplete; no matter how profound it might sound. Amen! Praying anything else may be the good and acceptable will of God our Father; yet without a "now" mindset of speaking the Kingdom within our midst; it is yet not the perfect will of God. (Romans 12:2). Jesus made it plain.

Say.... thy kingdom come, thy will be done on earth as it is in heaven

Firstly, because clearly the will of God is mostly not done on earth without declaration! To-**say- is to utter; to declare; to mouth** the words; for the tongue always gives power to our words whether for good or for evil. Everything which happens begins with words, and around conversation. Therefore, we are to open our mouths as kings who have dominion and authority! **The Kingdom of God always brings the will of God into manifestation.** Jesus told us to say: because we are kings who have been given dominion; and kings make declarations; and the words of a king hold much sway**.**

This shouldn't be surprising at all; for it is God's will from the beginning that His sons would be brokers of both the earthly and the heavenly realms. This is a great responsibility given to us as sons of God; as creative speaking spirits who manifest what we say!. Man was placed on earth to be an ambassador of, and for, the Kingdom of God: to speak on Yahweh's behalf as His earthly representative. It is not a new thing! The glory here is **that the will of God is only always done, where the Kingdom is manifested!**

Heaven is our Missions Control Center. Jesus is the ladder; and in Him we are constantly ascending and descending the heavens; with the promise of an open heaven. (John 1:51). As we see and receive, we ought open our mouth and declare it; thereby bringing into existence that which is done in heaven (2Cor. 4:13). For example: in the face of sickness and disease, we speak healing; in cases of poverty and lack, we bring provision; in the face of sadness and sorrows, we speak joy—all because our receivers are open to what happens in heaven.

Of course heaven does break forth within our midst, as we gather in His Name for sure! Without this declaration, things happen; but not always as they are in heaven, and mostly not to the measure of the power of our declaration! We too often say "the Lord's will be done" or **whatever God wants"- or "it is totally up to God"** as if it is some static thing which happens outside of us as Christians! That is not only being passive, and fatalistic; but it is being both ignorant and irresponsible; and unworthy of kings! To reiterate: **the will of God is always done where the Kingdom of God is manifested!**

Yahweh honored us with this privilege; because it pleased Him to do so. It is silly and unbiblical to just throw into the wind-so to speak; "the **Lord's will be done!** What Jesus told us in *Matthew 6:10* **"thy kingdom come, thy will be done on earth as it is in heaven"** is a gentle mandate! So, the concept of *on earth as it is in heaven* - **is important**!! Just ask most believers about their dreams and aspirations. You will more than likely get "the Lord's will be done" answer; or this>

"I'M WAITING ON THE LORD!"

Another very well-meaning saying. Bathed in ignorance, it often causes sweet, God-loving believers to lead fatalistic, mediocre lives unconsciously questioning God's love for them. After spending years and years in so called "waiting," many still haven't seen the promises of God, and like ancient Israel, too many Christians are perishing in the wilderness of the soul. Lack of proper knowledge and instruction in God's oracles. Oftentimes, believers begin to develop an "aught" against God; because after many years; they haven't gotten the answers they desired.

There is always the good, and the acceptable, will of God in all matters! "Waiting on the Lord" is one profound but too little understood precept within the Body of God's love! The Scripture is obviously not perverted, nor is it silly. The Word of God is true! Let us now begin to see the "perfected" will of God for us in this; for we are no longer mere children; but now are we the sons of Yah!

If you have been in church for any number of years, you undoubtedly have heard this beloved verse. I have also! However, not having received proper instructions regarding the blessedness and fullness of such a great verse; I also wandered for some years, **passively "waiting on the Lord,"** not really seeing changes in many situations. Like so many others; because we love God as much as we know how, I really did believe I was suffering for Jesus! Yet on a deeper level, I started to feel abandoned and rejected at times; and not unlike Eve; I often felt abandoned and like God was withholding something from me!

The picture of "waiting on the Lord" is one of radical, active faith; rather than merely sitting back while God does "His thing!"

98

Father does *work in us both to will and to do of His good pleasure Phil2:12.* Our Father is zealous of His grace and glory inside us; and He longs to see the fruit of His life flowing out from within us. Therefore, while we tend to focus on the destination, oftentimes impatiently; our Father is more passionate about our journey! He desires to enjoy us on the journey; as well as to have us really know and enjoy Him; while we are yet going through our "situation."

While you wait, there must be **a radical preparation taking place on your part; as you actively tend to the stewardship of your own soul!** The fruit of God's life must begin to be manifested from within you! Waiting is faithful preparation for the elevation which one knows by faith will follows! It is patiently enduring; as glory manifests from within!

Picture hunters in a forest filled with prey; guns in hand; cocked and ready, as they watch for their target! They are ready to pounce as the unknowing, unwitting prey approaches. This is the picture of waiting! **Waiting is not a fatalistic sitting down while expecting God to give us what we need.** Truth is He gives us faith to access the heavenly realms and our Heavenly Daddy brings things to us, and makes us aware of them! Then **He waits: He watches** us to see what we will do as He did with Adam. Picture Moses at the burning bush:

*And when the Lord saw that **Moses turned aside to see**; God called unto him from out of the midst of the bush! Exodus 3:4*

Yahweh spoke "when He saw Moses turn aside to see! How about that! Fast forward to Israel leaving the bondage of Egypt and facing the Red Sea, with Pharaoh's army fast approaching. Moses bravely declared to Israel that Yahweh would deliver them:

fear ye not, standstill and see the salvation of the Lord (Exo.14:13).

Moses must have been crying out in his heart to God for Yahweh answered him thus!

Why are you crying out to me? Speak unto the children of Israel that they go forward: but lift thou up thy rod and stretch out thine hand over the sea, and divide it. (Exodus14:15-16).

At Yahweh's instruction; Moses lifted up his rod and parted the sea! Moses's rod was the hand of God! Great picture of co-laboring with God, but that is Old Testament you say. Well, Jesus modeled it for us as well! One time the disciples were struggling against a horrible storm in their lives. They were rowing with no headway, while Jesus was actually in the boat with them, asleep. They cried:

Lord, carest not that we perish?" (Mark 4:38).

They cried out as if they were unsure if Jesus would indeed deliver them. That is so typical of us all! Christians carry Jesus in our spirits, yet we cry out at the slightest hint of a storm! The difference was that Jesus walked daily with the Father—fully knowing and completely assured that Father was with Him because He pleased the Father. He didn't have to constantly cry out and question His Father. Jesus slept on that boat; as a mirror for us that He knew about, and believed on, the Kingdom from which He came. He was not moved by what was going on!

His physical body was on the boat, but His mind was in the Kingdom of Heaven where there are no storms: for His, is a Kingdom of Peace! Then the son of man, being a broker of both realms, got up, opened His mouth; spoke to the storm and the storm obeyed His command! **Jesus stood up in the natural; spoke from the kingdom; exercised his authority as man; and brought the Kingdom of God to the earth realm.** That is what kings do! Jesus did not go pray; and He didn't go on a fast. He lived a fasted life of prayer. He basically released His faith and told the mountain to move, and it obeyed Him. That is for our example!

Our waiting on the Lord ought not be passive at all; neither should it be weak and wishy-washy! It is a virtual cocking of our spiritual guns, pouncing; and causing the effect that is needed. It is an expectant, faith-filled preparation and looking unto—to seize opportunities we know Yahweh will indeed open up for us!

Joseph dreamt a dream; and suffered many things when he told his dream to his family. Yet in whatever adverse circumstance he found himself; Joseph used his gifts and talents, and kept his dream ever before his face. He was filled with the Spirit of God and rose up to be the steward of his master's house. When he was thrown in prison Joseph interpreted the chief butler's dream and charged him to remember him when it went well with him (Gens 40:13-14). He worked with God even while waiting on God! Yet he had his own dream in sight, when he interpreted Pharaoh's dream by the Spirit of God. Then, he told Pharaoh:

look out a man discreet and wise and set him over the land of Egypt." (Gen. 41:33).

Joseph had been faithfully waiting on the Lord, and he was ready! Not **only did he interpret the dream; he also took dominion and exercised authority when he instructed Pharaoh on how to move forward!** He knew after interpreting that dream when all of Pharaoh's "wise men" had failed to do so; that he was the man! Surely, there were many men in Pharaoh's cabinet with MBA's and major degrees; but Joseph had been cocking his spiritual faith gun for years, and he was fully equipped, ready, and able. In faith he, *"shaved himself and changed his garments" Gens.41:14.*

Waiting on the Lord is a radical resting in love, actively knowing and declaring that Yahweh is at work! Joseph knew when to pounce! The door was open; and Joseph made sure to kick it wider! He never asked for time to go pray and sanctify a fast; to find out what the dream meant! He was ready! Radically ready! The command to *"look out a man discreet and wise and set him over the land of Egypt"* is not the talk of a prisoner. It is a king's command!

Now, we have been given the keys of the Kingdom of heaven at our disposal: we have the Word of God; the power of agreement and the power of binding and loosing (Matt,16:19). We have numerous pure and precious promises which have been given to us! We are understanding the power of the tongue— powerful principles and precepts! This is the faith which brings results! I ask you though; what have you been long waiting on the Lord for? Have you spent time and prepared: honing your skills, practicing your craft, and waited, watching with expectant eyes; as a hunter after prey?

Waiting on the Lord is aggressive, yet restful. It is an accepting of the finished work of the Cross! It is a powerful, methodical declaring of the Word of God, **not a resigned woeful hope.** It is more than hope—it is substance! The substance of kings! The substance of gods. Amen!

CHAPTER 22

FROM THE BEGINNING OF TIME

Yahweh's purposes have never changed: and they never will! He created man: male and female, and commanded them to be fruitful and multiply, and to replenish the Earth. Adam and Eve, even in the most perfect "garden" environment messed up. The couple had a family, and their son, Cain, killed his brother, Abel! Yahweh started over with another of Adam's son, in the godly line of Seth. In Seth's son Enos; men began to call upon the name of the Lord (Gens 4:26): and through the loins of Seth, He then found a man named Noah who was righteous in his generation.

When man became too wicked and multiplied upon the face of the Earth, Noah obeyed Yahweh; and built an Ark even when there was no rain. Yahweh flooded the Earth and started over with Noah and his family (Genesis 4:26:5-6). Noah's generation also messed up and Yahweh started over yet again. He chose a man called Abram, a heathen, to whom God gave a covenant promise that He would make of Abram a great nation (Gens.12:2,3). Abram obeyed God and left his country; his father's house and culture and began to walk with Yahweh by faith.

After a long while, Abram had not produced an heir, and so he enquired of Yahweh for an heir. Yahweh promised Abram that his descendants would be as innumerable as the stars in the heavens (Gens.15:5); and Abram believed in the Lord! Finally, Yahweh had a man! Yahweh renamed him Abraham, which means "father of many nations." Abraham and wife Sarah had a son Isaac, who had Jacob and Esau. Yahweh now had a family. Jacob (renamed Israel) had twelve sons; and out of the twelve sons arose the twelve tribes of Israel. And a nation was born!

Out of the nation of Israel, Yahweh chose one tribe, Judah; and through the loins of Judah, in King David, Yahweh brought forth His Son Jesus, of the root of Jesse and the offspring of David! Born of woman; son of man and son of God—related to Adam by race, related to Abraham in redemption and related to David in royalty. Then from His Son Jesus came every tribe, every tongue, and every nation! And the Church was born!

Yahweh is Father, because He has children! The very essence of our salvation is that in Jesus we now have been restored to the Father heart of God. Having been the first to see the resurrected Jesus at the tomb, Mary was told by Jesus:

But go to my brethren and say unto them, I ascend unto my Father and your Father, and to my God and your God. (John 20:17)

Jesus made us family! In the resurrection; Yahweh was now, not just our God; but He is now Father! Our Father! Firstly there was a man, who had a family; from that family came many tribes, then there was a nation. From that nation, the tribe of Judah produced the Christ! All have been instruments used by Yahweh to usher in His kingdom purposes in the Earth. From Jesus the Seed, the Christ; through the resurrection from the dead: there is the Body of Christ; a many-membered mystical body, called the Church! This is the family and household of God that the Apostle Paul prayed about in Ephesians 3:15. **The Church is that last instrument of God being used to usher in His Kingdom** (Ephesians 3:10).

For this cause, I bow my knees unto the Father of our Lord Jesus Christ, of whom the whole family in heaven and earth is named.

To the intent that now unto principalities and powers in heavenly places might be made known by the Church, the manifold wisdom of God!

It is for this purpose that Jesus the Christ was born! To establish His Father's kingdom on the Earth. Just as Yahweh demonstrated His might and power to Pharaoh; God is still waiting for His Church to show principalities and powers the many-sided wisdom of Yahweh. That the whole earth might know that Yahweh is God Almighty indeed! We declare that the Kingdom of God is here; now; among us! Amen and Amen!

CHAPTER 23

REPENTANCE

I n 2 Corinthians7:10, the Scriptures declares: *for godly sorrow worketh repentance to salvation not to be repented of..*

There is a great need to revisit repentance from a kingdom point of view and not just from a Church paradigm. While the Church is not in error, the subject is certainly in need of a fresh look. We have had a good, and an even acceptable understanding of God's will (Roms.12:2) as it pertains to repentance. In the Kingdom of Heaven though, we have the perfect will of God. Nonetheless, let us look at repentance through the eyes of the Gospel of Salvation. We have repented; for when we came to the Cross we turned from our sins towards God and we begin to experience being born again as the above Scripture states.

We are repenting as we daily work out our salvation; for we miss the mark;[often from ignorance]whether against God, or against man. Repentance is a gift from God; and an amazing space our Creator grants to us; in the face of shortcoming. The Hebrew word for repentance is "teshuva"; and it means "to return." **We come to Him; to our neighbors, sometimes to an enemy, and certainly to our brothers; and create new possibilities:** as we make right whatever offended! Repentance is a fruit of righteousness; and it is glorious!

Repent ye therefore, and be converted, that your sins might be blotted out, when the times of refreshing shall come from the presence of the Lord. And he shall send Jesus Christ who was before preached unto you.

Metanoeo" is greek for repentance, and it means to change one's mind. It involves a turning from wrong/sin/missing the mark and turning toward the Lord; to His precepts; His laws and statues. It involves your intellect, your emotions and your will. It is the picture of wanting to go southbound, yet you get on a bus going north. When you are aware (intellect) that you are headed in the wrong direction, your emotions are stirred; certainly, you feel sorry for getting on the wrong bus. However, until you get off that bus; which is an act of your will; then you are indeed still headed in the wrong direction!

As you work out your salvation; you are constantly repenting; from the perverse, the vile; the evil. Your salvation, is an ongoing process of getting the whole mind saved. For the most part, in Church we have preached repentance only as sorrow for sins; and obviously that is a beautiful thing! There is that personal repentance, which brings us personal revival (Acts 3:21). It does not necessarily mean you have sinned. As it daily relates to the Blood-washed believer, as new truths are understood; there is that godly sorrow which works repentance in us. As it might relate to the things of this book; in your repentance from missing the mark, it might involve turning away from the old; turning from the false; the vile, and the perverse.

We have repented, we are repenting, and we shall yet repent. As much as we have been given numerous valuable tools; we still "see through a glass darkly, (1Cor.13:12) There is also coming a day; at the appearing of Jesus Christ, that all of mankind will change our minds on some level; because that which is perfect will be before our eyes. That will be a great and awesome day indeed!

Beloved, now are we the sons of God, and it doth not yet appear what we shall be: but we know that, when He shall appear, we shall be like Him; for we shall see His as He is. 1John 3:2

Therefore, judge nothing before the time, until the Lord come. Who both will bring to light the hidden things of darkness, and will make manifest the counsels of the hearts; and then shall every man have praise of God. (1Cor.4:5).

Thus, there are layers of truth to the concept of repentance. I invite you to look at an even deeper paradigm of repentance! From the Paradigm of the Kingdom of Heaven…as Jesus taught it!

CHAPTER 24

REPENT: FOR THE KINGDOM
OF HEAVEN IS AT HAND

John the Baptist **burst out of the wilderness preaching** *"Repent ye: for the kingdom of heaven is at hand."* (Matthew 3:2) It was a radical message that had not been heard up until then, and many folks pressed into the kingdom. Jesus came to John to be baptized; and His Father openly validated Him as His Beloved Son before all who were present (Matt.3:16,17). After His baptism, He was immediately led into the wilderness for forty days of severe temptation and buffeting, during which time he fasted and prayed to His father.

Having overcome the evil one, and having been ministered to by angels, Jesus comes out of the wilderness in the power of the Holy Spirit and, of course, He goes to Temple, as was His norm. He opened the book to, and then quoted Isaiah 61:1-2 (Luke 4:18-19); validating His Father's approval and anointing! He was ready for ministry! Jesus entered the scene declaring the Kingdom paradigm. **He began preaching,** *Repent: for the kingdom of heaven is at hand."* (Matthew 4:17) mirroring the same message which John had been preaching:

It wasn't just a message of repent because of [your] sins! Rather it was **"repent for-the-kingdom"** was now here. Allow me to paraphrase the messages they preached. It involves a change of your mind concerning the way you have been looking at your life, relationships; situations; as well as your perception of Yahweh, His law and statues; and certainly your perception of Heaven. What was available only in types and shadow; is now available to you and for you; in the Person of Jesus. Sin's solution was finally here!

106

When Adam sinned in the garden of God; Yahweh killed an animal and covered the couple with an animal's skin. That was the first time in the Bible that blood had been physically shed. The animal's skin however, only covered the body! Yahweh was stating the obvious when He killed that first animal: that sin had to be covered, or atoned for! Then in Lev.17:11 God gave us the precept for what He had done in Eden. We are told:

For the life of the flesh (soul) is in the blood: and I have given it to you upon the altar to make atonement for your souls; for it is the blood that maketh atonement for the soul. Amen.

As a result, the shedding of blood was required under the Old Covenant. The priests had to sprinkle blood on every piece of furniture and ornament in the Tabernacle; [a type of Jesus Christ]. For there could be no semblance of soul in anything Yahweh was involved in; only spirit! In the garden of God; spirit never sinned; but the soul did: and had pre-empted spirit as ruler.

the soul that sinneth, it shall die Ezekiel 18:20 states.

For this reason, the carnal man/soul, is always at enmity against God (Roms.8:6-8)! Soul could no longer have any say; and for ages to come; man had to make atonement for the soul by the blood covering of animals! Until Jesus! In Jesus; there is no semblance of the soul ruling; for Jesus; *the last Adam was made a quickening [life giving] spirit (1Cor.15:45).*

Yahweh throughout the ages had purposed all things in Himself through His Son Jesus the Resurrection! This mystery had been hid in God throughout the ages. The mind of God had His very own Son crucified; as a conciliatory sacrifice to God Almighty. Now Jesus the sacrificial Lamb was here: manifested in the flesh; and no longer was there a need to cover for sin! For in Jesus there was now:

the New Testament in [my] blood, which is shed for you. Luke22:20

Jesus's message that the Kingdom of Heaven was now here is both powerful and encompassing. **Although Jesus never said salvation is here; the Kingdom of Heaven comes equipped with salvation in the remittance of sin.** Salvation is the prerequisite for the Kingdom; and Jesus told Nicodemus:

except a man be born again he cannot see the kingdom."

Salvation involves the shedding of Jesus blood! The writer of Hebrews and the Apostle Paul declares' that the blood of bulls and goats could not take away sin. That was imperfect, and so they could only cover sin. **But Jesus's blood, shed on Calvary remitted our sins!** John the Baptist when he saw first Jesus made this declaration

Behold the Lamb of God which taketh away the sin of the world. John 1:29.

The Kingdom of Heaven is now here and can be accessed! Jesus promised us that He would drink wine with us in the Kingdom, for wine is symbolic of blood. Deuteronomy 32:14 tell us

...and thou didst drink the pure blood of the grape

Wine is the blood of the grapes; and the grape is the wineskin. Jesus being the perfect sacrifice; took and lifted the cup of wine in communion with His disciples and symbolically stated:

This is my blood of the new covenant, which is shed for many for the remission of sins. Matt.26:28. Amen!

POWER PRINCIPLES OF THE KINGDOM OF HEAVEN

Jesus is the new wineskin; which carry new wine [blood]; a better blood, a better covenant. This was now available to us.

And to Jesus, the mediator of the new covenant, and to the blood of sprinkling that speaketh better things than the blood of Abel! Heb.9:12-14.

The Kingdom of Heaven comes with power and demonstration of Holy Spirit! The blood of Jesus made way for the third Person of the Godhead. In the Old Covenant Holy Spirit was only seen in types and shadows.Individuals had to be anointed by Holy Spirit for specific works or ministry, but there was no indwelling of the Holy Spirit in the spirits of men. **Now through Jesus's blood; Holy Spirit our Comforter, has come to powerfully indwell the spirits of man; bringing the Kingdom of Heaven through the water and the Spirit**. (Jn.3:4-5). Holy Spirit came as a permanent abode within the hearts of men as helper and Comforter, and now full access was made into God's Kingdom (Roms.14:17; Luke17:20-21).

Man was now empowered by Holy Spirit to live lives of authority and dominion. Not only did we receive salvation: now our intimacy with the Creator was restored! We knew Him as God; but now we could call Him Father (John 20:17). For the Father sent the spirit of the Son in our heart crying Abba, [Daddy] Father (Gals.6:6). **In Holy Spirit; through the Son, we have received the spirit of adoption; now we can call God, Daddy** (Roms.8:15)! And Holy Spirit shed abroad in our hearts the love of God, the Father (Roms.5:5). **Now we can have intimate fellowship with all Three persons of the Godhead in Holy Romance! GLORY!**

Thus the Kingdom comes equipped with all that is needed; Holy Ghost power and authority; healing, cleansing, deliverance, peace, joy, intimacy and so much more. Much more than just salvation! Repentance-for-the kingdom is paramount, and involves a radical paradigm shift! For it is possible for one to miss what was now available to man here on earth, right under one's nose, as Israel did! The Kingdom of Heaven is encompasses all, and is easily accessed! It is for these reasons that you need to:

repent for the kingdom of heaven...

The *"kingdom of heaven is at hand"* is a prophetic statement: that Jesus the King was here to recover His Kingdom! Not only was it in the future in His impending death and resurrection: but it was available now! Martha believed in the coming resurrection; yet in Jesus her brother Lazarus lived; for Jesus is indeed the Resurrection and the life of God out Father (John 11;23-25)!

"the kingdom of heaven is at hand;" it is within reach of one's hand; although not visible to the naked eye! Yet it is here, among us; and all around us; in another realm: in spirit (Roms.14:17)! One can easily bring it into this realm, through declaration. The message is, *"Thy kingdom come. Thy will be done in earth, as it is in heaven* (Matthew 6:10). You are now a broker of the heavenly realms when you SAY it!

With Jesus's ascension to the right hand of Majesty, we are called to bring the Kingdom of God to the earth, all the times, and for every situation! Jesus went about mirroring how to bring heaven into our everyday reality. He healed the sick, cleansed the lepers, opened blind eyes, cast out devils and raised the dead. Then He sent out seventy and told them to *"heal the sick that are therein and say: 'the kingdom of God is come nigh unto you"* (Luke10:9). He told His disciples **"preach saying the kingdom of heaven is at hand, heal the sick, cleanse the lepers, raise the dead, cast out** devils. (Matthew 10:8). Hallelujah!

Jesus lived an overcoming life in deep intimate fellowship with His and our Father. He declared: *"I and the Father are One" (John5:19);* and that *"the Father hath not left me alone; for I always do those things that pleases Him."* Jesus lovingly declared, *"I go to prepare a place for you that where I am, there ye may be also" (John 14: 2-3)!* How Beautiful!

Repenting because of sin is a truth given to the Church: it is both good and acceptable. It doesn't show the full counsel of God however. Jesus's message concerning repentance is the perfected will of His and our Father! It is so powerful! You repent so you can see the solution to your sins, as well as live kingly lives on earth as if you were living in heaven. God had come to live among His people in the Tabernacle of Moses. **Post resurrection, the Holy Spirit has come; dwelling in our hearts (Luke 17:21) through His Son; ushering His supernatural kingdom and giving us both love, power and sound minds** (2 Tim.1:7)! Holy Spirit empowers us also, to live kingly lives of authority and dominion.

The Church has done a fantastic job of preaching "the gospel of salvation." Phenomenal amounts of souls have been radically saved, and are still being saved! This is the good, and definitely the acceptable will of God. Too many believers however, once saved have stayed camped out; waiting to be taken out of the earth; and **have thus lost vision of the power of the Kingdom**! Meanwhile leading very mediocre infantile lives; believers have languished too often below their ordained power and authority; barely tolerating those wretched "sinners" until that day of the Church's "Rapture."

Because believers haven't been living as kings; it is **easier to blame the enemy rather than stand up and "declare" the finished work of Christ!** These same believers have too often remained infantile in nature and behavior, ignorant of the mandate to steward the earth; and the responsibility of saving the soul by renewing the mind. These are people who love Jesus; and are faithful to Him; yet are unlearned and untrained for kingdom rule.

Jesus told many different fabulous stories of His Father's coming kingdom; He painted vivid pictures of how one qualifies for and grows in the kingdom. He gave us the laws of the Kingdom in the Beatitudes (Matt.5); taught us the priority of the Kingdom; showed us in the parable of the sower; (Matt.13:18-23) and qualified the kingdom heart progression. Many, many principles, and precepts; hidden in the wisdom of God! He declared Himself the *"way, the truth and the life,"* and He left us the Book with much immutable evidence. Yet there is such a searing lack of kingdom understanding in the Body of Christ! And it is the one thing satan is scared of believers understanding! Jesus' message on the kingdom state:

When anyone hears the word of the kingdom and understandeth it not, then cometh the evil one and catcheth away that which was sown in his heart. (Matt.13:19)

It is expedient that the Gospel of the Kingdom of Heaven which was heralded by both Jesus and John, be preached in every sphere so believers might daily access this marvelous Kingdom! It is the one fundamental way that we are destroyed [perishing] due to a lack of knowledge! As a result of that, we have been missing the power, the authority, the resource, and the purpose of God's heart in the Earth.

And no man putteth new wine into old bottles; else the new wine will burst the bottles, and be spilled, and the bottles shall perish.

But new wine must be put into new bottles, and both are preserved.

No man also having drunk old wine straightway desireth new: for he saith, the old is better. Luke 5:37-39).

Since the Church is the last instrument of God being used to further the cause of the Kingdom; this book is a voice crying in the wilderness! There is a mighty kingdom to be had, here on Earth! We are sky walkers; made to sit together in heavenly places with Christ!

Lord, we confess that we have been ignoring the message of the Kingdom of Heaven. We repent, and humbly cry out for deeper understanding of this power Oracle. Forgive us Father!

CHAPTER 25

REALIGNING WITH
THE KINGDOM OF GOD/HEAVEN!

T he terms, the Kingdom of Heaven and the Kingdom of God are actually used by Jesus the King Himself, over a hundred times in the Gospels, while Jesus mentions the word Church a mere three times. In the Church world however, the opposite is apparent: the message of salvation is preached, while the kingdom message is scarcely mentioned. You can easily sit in too many local churches for a full year or more, and never hear the word **Kingdom of God** even being uttered! Mostly, preachers seem to have ignored the responsibility of teaching the message of the Kingdom of Heaven, although that was all Jesus talked about.

The message of personal salvation is needed on one level, for you are called to *work out your own salvation with fear and trembling* (Phil.2:12-13). That is needed, but not to the exclusion of the kingdom message. Matter of truth; it is included in the kingdom message. For we walk with each other in the Kingdom of God; and every joint supplies. (Eph.4:16) Father made that very clear! Yet, without embracing the focal message Jesus preached, we no doubt have miss the greater purpose Yahweh intended. Matthew 6:33 says

seek ye first the kingdom of God and His righteousness…

To seek means: **"attempt to find!"** This ought to be first! There is a kingdom available; and it is a mystical one! Amen.

Even the mystery which has been hid from ages and generations, but now is made manifest to His saints: to whom God would make known, what is the riches of the glory of this mystery among the Gentiles; which is Christ in you the hope of glory. (Col.1:27).

112

The glory of any kingdom is its citizens. The hope Yahweh has, includes the beauty of His sons and daughters in the courts of the Kingdom of God! God's kingdom glory is a people who think like Him; with His desires, His mindset; His wants. His sons are His glory! Jesus answered Pilates's question whether He was a king:

To this end was I born, and for this reason came I into the world (John 18:36)

Jesus died for this! Without embracing the kingdom paradigm, believers tend to focus only on making a quick exit from this present evil world; while leading mostly mediocre lives in the now. We can miss the beauty of God's heart for His sons; so it is for this that we must shift our paradigm in order to truly capture and embrace this reality! Jesus's message is much bigger than being only about personal salvation.

We are called to rule on earth; and to be in training to reign with Jesus in His millennial kingdom! It is about Yahweh's heart and Eternal purposes. It is therefore expedient that our perceptions, ideas, thoughts, concepts; the whole mindset: **be transformed from being just about personal salvation to being Kingdom purposed!** This is the full counsel of Yah! We must look at everything from Heaven's viewpoint: how the Kingdom of God is being impacted all around; for we are all collectively a part of the greater whole; and it is glorious! This is how we dress and keep the earth. Amen

The whole world needs to hear the message of the Kingdom of Heaven! Jesus told us *"this gospel of the kingdom shall be preached in all the world for a witness unto all nations; and then the end will come"* (Matthew 24:14). The Church, being the last process being used by Yahweh to further His kingdom in the Earth, must get on with the business of preaching the kingdom message. We have been called and commissioned by Jesus Himself, to view all aspect of life from God's Eternal purposes, His Glory and His soon coming kingdom! Repentance is thus needed, to refine our collective focus.

That will require a deeper knowledge of the ways of the King of Heaven; and a deeper revelation of the Father Heart of God, for that is Who Yahweh is—He is Father! We absolutely must understand and know how to keep satan in his proper place as a defeated foe, cast down to the Earth, the one for whom an eternal hell has been prepared! Amen! That too, is a part of our kingdom responsibility! This will become established as the Church acquires more of the knowledge and fear of Yahweh, as well as when we wash out our collective mouth with soap. We must stop ignoring what Jesus says concerning His kingdom and embrace our Father's intention.

Come ye blessed of my Father, inherit the kingdom prepared for you from the foundation of the world. Matthew 25:34

Once we grab hold of the promises of God by radical faith, we can hasten the day (2 Pet 3:12), and we *can taste of the power of the worlds to come (Hebrews 6:5).* The Canaanite woman in her desperation, pressed into Jesus for the healing of her daughter. (Matt.15:22-28). The centurion did as well! They knew nothing of the resurrection; yet both believed, and they received. They came to Jesus, as we do in prayer; and then left with the results they needed because of the manner in which they moved God through faith.

Jesus demonstrated that His kingdom might be accessed at any given moment; when He declared in John 11:25 **"I Am the Resurrection and the life…"** Our heavenly Father and Daddy desires for us to access it every day, every minute; by declaring it with our mouths! It is our kingly duty and responsibility! We must "sell" all of our carnal ideas, concepts, thoughts and opinions and rid ourselves of stinking thinking! We must so totally embrace [buy] the Kingdom of Heaven; that nothing else will suffice! It is to this end that Scriptures tells us;

The kingdom of heaven is like unto treasure hid in a field; the which when a man hath found, he hideth, and for joy thereof goeth and selleth all that he hath, and buyeth that field. (Matt.13:44)

Again, the kingdom of heaven is like unto a merchant man, seeking goodly pearls: Who when he found one pearl of great price, went and sold all that he had, and bought it. (Matthew 13:45-46).

Father, let your Kingdom come; let Your will be done, here, on earth as it is done in Heaven!

For Thine is the kingdom, and the power and the glory! Amen!

www.ingramcontent.com/pod-product-compliance
Lightning Source LLC
Chambersburg PA
CBHW070812050426
42452CB00011B/2010